EXPLODING
DATA

EXPLODING DATA

RECLAIMING OUR CYBER SECURITY IN THE DIGITAL AGE

MICHAEL CHERTOFF

Atlantic Monthly Press

New York

FIRST EDITION

Published simultaneously in Canada
Printed in the United States of America

First Grove Atlantic hardcover edition: July 2018

Library of Congress Cataloging-in-Publication data is available for this title.

ISBN 978-0-8021-2793-8
eISBN 978-0-8021-6578-7

Atlantic Monthly Press
an imprint of Grove Atlantic
154 West 14th Street
New York, NY 10011

Distributed by Publishers Group West

groveatlantic.com

18 19 20 21   10 9 8 7 6 5 4 3 2 1

For Meryl, Emily, and Philip,
and for those who serve . . .

CONTENTS

EXPLODING
DATA

INTRODUCTION

BIG DATA IS
WATCHING YOU

O N THE MORNING OF SEPTEMBER 11, 2001, while I drove to my Washington, D.C., office as assistant U.S. attorney general in charge of the Department of Justice Criminal Division, my deputy called to tell me that an airplane had crashed into New York City's World Trade Center. Our initial assumption was that a private-plane pilot had lost his way. But within minutes, the TV news reported a second plane had smashed into the twin towers. That's when we realized America was under attack.

Within minutes we were at the FBI Strategic Information and Operation Center, working with the FBI director to piece together who was attacking us and—importantly— how to prevent further strikes. As we began to pull together the facts, we learned a third aircraft had crashed into the Pentagon. A fourth plane, United Flight 77, had also been hijacked and was headed to Washington, D.C. The order was relayed to fighter jets to shoot down the plane; that became unnecessary after the passengers heroically stormed the cockpit and forced down the jet in Shanksville, Pennsylvania. America was at war.

Over the next hours and days, we pieced together the identities of the hijackers and concluded that al Qaeda was carrying out its declaration of war against America. Shortly after the attacks, President George W. Bush told the attorney general, "Don't let this happen again." That became our mandate.

This war was different from previous conflicts. Our enemies wore no uniforms and flew no flags; they sought to sneak up on us in the guise of ordinary civilians. Their weapons were homemade explosives. They mingled with the flow of travelers. Against this concealed attacker, radar that we relied upon to warn against enemy missiles or bombers was of no use.

How, then, to detect other terrorists and prevent them from carrying out attacks? We quickly concluded the answer lay in collecting large amounts of information about travelers and foreigners, and discerning the connections and behavior that showed links to a terror network. That meant not only reorienting our intelligence agency to focus on detecting the outlines of the terror network, but also obtaining the capability to detect patterns in the vast amounts of data being collected.

This paradigm shift in national security coincided with the expansion of the internet and the growth of commercial enterprises devoted to using data analytics for marketing and credit-scoring purposes. The private sector, infused with the urgency of preventing further attacks, began to develop new strategies to find the terrorist needle in the haystack. As the same time, the intelligence community expanded our data haystacks, using new or repurposed legal authorities (including the USA PATRIOT Act, which I participated in drafting) to accumulate information about the global flow of money, people, and communications. Over the next several years, as head of the Department of Justice's Criminal Division and later as U.S. secretary of homeland security, I saw the awesome power of expanded data collection and analytics as tools to protect our nation and its people.

Not surprisingly, these new capabilities began to be deployed for other purposes, including commercial objectives. Just as the civilian internet was spawned by a Defense Department research effort, data collection and analytic tools used in counterterrorism were applied for a host of commercial purposes. Because I was witness to a major turning point in the growth of increasingly pervasive surveillance and the revolution in data collection, storage, and analysis—called "big data" by many—I was acutely aware of the power of data collection and analytics to benefit society. I also knew this information-gathering revolution would challenge America's traditional notions and values in the areas of privacy and liberty.

As time has passed, I have been professionally and personally involved in guiding, prompting, using, and worrying about the ever-expanding harvesting of personal data by both governments and, even more so, the private sector. Perhaps more than most, I understand how much data each of us now generates for collection. That can be beneficial. It can also be very dangerous.

Having spent most of my professional career as a lawyer and as a judge, I am also mindful that our legal rules and policies established how these vast new capabilities would be deployed; yet most of this legal framework was created in the 20th century, when the data landscape was far sparser than it is today. As one who wants to encourage the positive effects of the data revolution, I believe that we are overdue to recast the rules of the road. To be sure, this data revolution should preserve, rather than undermine, our fundamental values.

This book is designed to educate the interested citizen about the scope and implications of the revolution in data generation, collection, and analytics. I also lay out a vision to retain the security and economic benefits of these developments without unwittingly sacrificing our privacy, liberty, and civic values. To illustrate how rapidly this change is coming upon us, here are four hypothetical but realistic scenarios—three of which are already upon us.

One: A young New Yorker, Alan, becomes interested in the ideology of radical jihadism. After searching the internet, he happens upon a website managed by recruiters for a terrorist organization in Syria. The terrorists detect Alan's interest and make contact with him by sending an email to his Internet Protocol (IP) address with instructions on how to anonymize communications by downloading free software. With excitement, he steps into the shadows.

Although Alan follows the jihadis' instructions, he also begins to discuss his increasing radicalization with friends on Facebook. He posts pictures of himself with a beard and wearing a *thobe*, the traditional robe worn in many Arab countries.

He discusses his developing political views with his friends. He also visits websites that instruct viewers on how to build a bomb using household products and chemicals that can be easily purchased in gardening stores. At one point, Alan goes online to explore travel routes to Syria, although he does not buy a ticket. Ben, a friend of Alan's who has in fact traveled to Syria, phones him on several occasions to encourage him to come. Alan responds by email in veiled language that he intends to carry out a task in the United States that will be "heavenly." Alan also visits a local gardening superstore, buying quantities of chemicals greater than would normally be used for hobby gardening in New York City.

Unbeknownst to Alan, intelligence and law enforcement officials monitoring transnational communications, both telephone and internet, have detected his contact with Ben. But these officials do not intercept the content of the two men's communication in real time. Because Syria is a known terrorist area of operation, the authorities seek permission from a special federal judge to collect as much information as possible about Alan's communications. As soon as they can, the Feds want to determine whether Alan poses a threat.

Specifically, they want to subpoena metadata—email records with numbers or IP addresses—showing Alan's contacts for the last two years; the Feds also want to obtain records of online tweets and social media postings by Alan, as well as records of his online searches and website visits. The federal agents also subpoena his credit card records.

Examining this data reveals most of Alan's online and communications activity for many months. At the same time, application of analytic algorithms to this huge cache of data yields an outline of Alan's evolving extreme views. He has made efforts to travel to Syria, an overseas terrorist hotbed. Alan has made contact with identifiable terrorists and researched bomb-making techniques. His credit card records show the alarming accumulation of chemicals that correlate to the bomb-making instructions on the website Alan visited.

The agents go further. Contacting the NYPD, they obtain several months of footage from video cameras positioned in lower Manhattan's financial district. Although the volume of this footage is far too great for human eyes to review, video analytic tools with facial-recognition capability quickly identify that in the last two months Alan has been loitering near the Federal Reserve building in New York.

Based on this information, the authorities manufacture a persuasive cover story that permits an undercover agent to befriend Alan by pretending to be a violent extremist. The agent gains Alan's confidence by expressing views strikingly similar to those Alan has expressed online. Eventually, Alan reveals to him the intent to carry out a bombing at the Federal Reserve. Alan is arrested.

Two: Brian and Kate are shopping for a birthday present for their six-year-old daughter, Ashley. At one store, they encounter Talkie Terry, a doll whose ability to listen and respond to human speech is "so lifelike that your child will have a new friend." As explained by Omnicorp, the manufacturer, Terry is able to recognize speech and instantly relay it wirelessly to a server housing thousands of potential responses to any request or statement a child makes.

Moreover, Terry's server retains a file on past interactions with each child, so Terry gets to "know" the child—Terry will be able to remind Ashley of past events, make suggestions, and even initiate conversation. Omnicorp touts Terry as a learning tool. Terry will encourage children to learn a language, do chores, and appreciate moral lessons. Even better, parents can link Terry to their smartphones with an app, so they can monitor the child's activities in the vicinity of Terry, since the doll is never really turned "off."

Best of all, Terry is inexpensive—not surprising when you realize that the doll's real value is in the vast amount of data it collects for Omnicorp to use in other business activities, including mail-order retail, financial services, and information brokering.

Indeed, Ashley's conversation, and all conversation within earshot of Terry's sensitive and always operational microphone, is not only retained on Omnicorp's server but also mined by algorithms, revealing a good deal of information about this family's plans and preferences. When Brian links Terry to his smartphone, it plants a cookie to monitor the websites he visits. And the next version of Terry will be even better, with the capability to emit an ultrahigh-frequency sound wave—inaudible to humans—that links up with other "smart" devices in the household, like a web-enabled television. Terry will let Omnicorp record what the family members watch on television as well as other data about their lives.

All of this is, of course, fully disclosed in the 75-page "terms and conditions of use" consent form that Brian clicked on when he connected Terry to the internet. Brian was far too busy trying to set up the doll for his excited daughter to carefully read the form. And once Brian brought the doll home for Ashley, was he really going to disappoint his daughter by taking it back?

Talkie Terry is modeled on My Friend Cayla, a doll banned by German authorities as an illegal eavesdropping device. Cayla records speech and can be accessed via Bluetooth. Other internet-connected toys include Mattel's Hello Barbie.[1]

Three: Carl is a young assistant professor who teaches privacy law, and, of course, he prides himself on vigilantly guarding his own privacy. Carl does not have a personal social media site and is careful about what he tweets. He does not visit websites that require you to download cookies that track online behavior. He uses an encrypted email service and does not authorize the service provider to mine his email for personal data. Carl feels he is prudent about the amount of personal data he allows others to access.

But Carl enjoys modern "smart" technology and unwittingly leaves quite a bit of digital exhaust.[2] A typical day begins when his alarm goes off, and its wireless connection to the coffeemaker turns on the brew cycle. Carl checks the Fitbit around his wrist to see how well he slept. That data, along with how many steps he takes today and what his heart rate is, will be continuously uploaded to his smartphone.

For breakfast, Carl makes himself a big meal of bacon and eggs. He uses the smart refrigerator to update his connected shopping list with bacon and a few other supplies; an order is automatically placed with a local grocer to deliver a quantity that approximates the current rate at which he indulges. In his car, Carl buckles up, automatically engaging his GPS and emergency communications link, as well as his internet-based radio. To save money, Carl has also signed up for an insurance-based device that records his driving behavior. These devices relay to his insurer the information that Carl tends to abruptly accelerate and decelerate, and that his typical driving route to work takes him on streets with a higher-than-average incidence of traffic accidents.

After a day of teaching, Carl uses his smartphone to add to his week's grocery list, begun earlier at home on the refrigerator panel. After buying the items on his shopping-list app, he recalls that he is due that evening at a farewell reception for a colleague at a local bar. Using his phone as a navigation device, Carl stops in for a drink, and his colleague snaps some smartphone photos of Carl at the party. These photos automatically upload to the colleague's social media account.

Soon after, Carl gets into his car and heads home.

That evening, Carl watches the news and a political-satire show on his web-enabled television. The high-definition TV automatically turns on when Carl enters the room, and can "suggest" viewing options based on his viewing preferences. The service provider can also record anytime Carl enters or leaves the room, and even when his attention shifts from the screen to something else in the room. Also, ultrahigh-frequency sound waves emitted by the television[3]—at a pitch inaudible to humans—automatically pair Carl's smartphone to his television,[4] recording when Carl searches on his phone for an item just advertised on the television.[5] New analytic software actually allows the service provider to determine whether Carl likes or dislikes what he is viewing based upon microscopic eye movements picked up by his smartphone that correlate with positive or negative reactions.[6]

Carl's health insurer later raises his premium because his eating, drinking, exercise, and sleep patterns could be healthier. The insurer suggests that a change in his diet and more exercise will trigger a special "healthy lifestyle" discount that will lower his rates. This is presented as a positive "nudge" toward reducing illness. His auto insurer also informs Carl that his rates will rise because his driving style is erratic, and he has been linked via social media to drinking establishments just before driving his vehicle. Commercial marketers send Carl advertising material based on preferences established from his stream of digital exhaust. Election-campaign specialists target him with ads based upon a behavioral analysis of Carl's reaction to news events and political commentary.

All the features in Carl's story currently exist. Progressive Insurance "rewards" drivers who install a monitoring device in their automobiles. One employer pays a bonus to employees who get seven hours of sleep a night, as recorded on their tracking devices. Eye-tracking technologies are currently being piloted on video systems.[7]

Four: James's eyes pop open, prying his thoughts from slumber. Once again, he has woken up at 5:43 a.m. James always does. The monitor never lets him linger in bed. He sometimes wonders what the early-21st-century "snooze function" might have been like. He has never experienced such a thing but has seen it in a few old movies. In modern

2084, the ideas of the previous century have not been deemed relevant and most of the media has been destroyed.

James has no such luxury. At the optimal awakening time, the monitor, already aware of his sleep phase, begins playing sounds to generate his awakening. The audible portions are supposed to be relaxing. James has chosen beach waves that remind him of his childhood on Cape Cod. Nearly inaudible portions connect with his subconscious, causing his body to begin waking whether he wants to or not.

Today he gets up quickly. Previously, the monitor's neural scan of James determined that he had been too slow in pulling out of a deep sleep, so it has increased the amount of subliminal communication. James doesn't know what it would be like to wake up late; the thought is so foreign to his prescribed daily routine that it occurred to him only after he had seen one of those old movies.

After James showers and makes his way toward the kitchen, the monitor presents him with three healthy breakfast options matching his weight, age, and health history. He is glad that he is still young enough to be allowed bacon, and he chooses a breakfast burrito heavy in kale and infused with egg whites. If he eats more than what is presented, the questioning begins. The same thing happens if James refuses to eat. The last time he attempted to skip breakfast, the monitor had detected his failure to accumulate the necessary caloric intake and, since this information was coupled with the fact that his daily bloodwork showed a rise in his white blood cell count, James was deemed too ill to work and was sent to bed.

Entering his travel pod, he begins his commute to the office.

Upon James's arrival, he is greeted by the monitors stationed outside the building, "Welcome, James Jones. The morning meeting begins at 9:00 in conference room B. Six out of eight attendees have arrived and are stationed in the room. Marcos is 2 minutes and 46 seconds away from arrival."

"Chipped" at birth, James is accustomed to having his location known and available to others. Initially developed as an expensive and optional parental security feature to ensure that rescue would be quick in case of kidnapping or accident, the chips were eventually demanded by everyone. Mass production and government help have made them affordable. Because of their usefulness in convicting criminals, society has come to accept them. Therefore, anyone who wants to find James can do so. As a by-product of the chip, his life's history can be played out as a simple series of circular patterns that rarely shift. It isn't as if he consciously thinks about it. His behavior morphed because he just doesn't want to be part of the interrogation that inevitably comes if he happens to be in the wrong place at the wrong time. Life is easier if his transit patterns match what is expected.

Although he already knows everyone in the conference room, as James enters, his "eyeglass" implants identify each participant by name. Although this technology is relatively new, James still finds it odd to view the world in "assisted mode." As he scans the room, an indicator showing each person's name is tagged in his vision. If he desires, James could probe for more information—his colleagues' education and work background, intelligence score, family members, and even medical history—by accessing the visual internet database.

After first receiving his eyeglass, James had regularly gone back to review meetings from his colleague Amy's perspective, hoping he might catch how often she had glanced his way. At first, she was stealing quick looks. She stopped doing this when the monitor flagged her viewing patterns as being irrelevant and a waste of corporate resources. James thinks Amy might be interested in him, but it is too hard to find a legitimate reason to reach out to her. Eventually, he gives up.

Crime rates have fallen tremendously. It is too hard to do something illegal when the crime is almost always captured by either an eyeglass or one of the scanning monitors installed as part of every streetlight. Homeowners installed their own scanning monitors when criminals began to target homes without such devices. The monitors proliferated, and on a vast scale. It wasn't mandated; it was as if the network spread on its own.

The dramatic drop in crime rates is due to not only the increased surveillance but also the increased ability of the organization to predict bad thoughts, ideas, and ultimately actions. This started as an improvement to the archaic lie-detector testing. Eye movements were first mapped to speech. This data was then processed with behavior recorded by the myriad sensors and video cameras throughout the city. From this data, predictive analytics are able to identify predisposition to erratic and even dangerous behavior.

Thoughts that cross a high negative threshold are automatically reported to the police.

James shakes himself out of his daydream. He isn't sure if the authorities can piece together his random thoughts into a coherent stream, but he does not doubt for a second that he is being monitored. Unsure of what thoughts might trigger a report to the police, James finds it simpler to focus only on the task at hand. Friends are a distraction, and he always ends up wondering which one of them is an agent. James wonders about just what is, no longer about what might be.

Each preceding scenario shows the revolutionary impact of universal data collection and analysis on people in the current day or the not-too-distant future. The first three are based on current technologies; the fourth is a dramatization of where they might lead. If the fourth scenario seems far-fetched, consider the combination of things already on the market or in development: facial recognition, automated cars, pervasive closed-circuit TV in many cities, and some companies' use of bird's-eye cameras overlooking workstations and voluntary (so far) microchips implanted in employees.[8] Of course, the effects of using any one of these devices may be good or bad. Unfortunately, too often government policy-makers, judges, and everyday consumers poorly understand the consequences of the big data revolution.

The effects of big data collection are playing out faster today than ever before. Information sharing has allowed new technologies to be created at an ever-faster pace. Technologies designed for security and classified by governments now quickly find their way into everyday consumers' hands. The commercial drive to enhance marketing tools also drives relentless innovation in the ability to collect and exploit data. Because today's information and networks have so many connection points, it is harder and harder to prevent information from leaking. Information doesn't disappear readily—it sticks. Taken together, these features of modern information technology have sped up the spread of ideas and our personal information.

As an unintended by-product, however, growing interconnectivity has had the effect of dramatically increasing threats to our security and privacy. The proliferation of wirelessly connected devices—often mobile—expands the surface area of network entry points through which hackers can penetrate our information and communication networks. By the same token, the centralized collection of our personal data by government and corporations means it is far easier for hackers to steal that data at a huge scale. So, consider the following recent cyber data threats: Equifax, the credit agency, loses data pertaining to 143 million Americans; Yahoo has 3 billon users' accounts compromised; and the U.S. Office of Personnel Management, the government's human resources agency, has highly sensitive security files relating to over 25 million employees and applicants stolen, perhaps by a foreign nation.

History does show that technological changes bring with them social and normative changes, allowing societies to adapt. So, the development of the automobile led to the adoption of safety requirements and the regulation of traffic patterns. Because in modern democracies people ultimately define the rules that determine or restrict their behavior—the social contract—the rules must adjust to meet the needs of the day. But new technology doesn't always fit within the existing social construct. Trying to force it into an outdated legal system may even break the system. Eventually people react by demanding fundamental changes to the rules. It falls to elected officials, administrators, and courts to recognize changed circumstances and then reconstruct legal and policy standards.

As the social contract is renegotiated, a return to basic principles and values is necessary. Standing outside the outmoded paradigms and automated legal categories, we must redetermine what our core social and ethical values are. What's in danger and what needs protection? Often the constitutional principles of liberty, security, freedom of expression and association, and independence must be weighed against each other, possibly with the interests of society balanced against the rights and interests of the individual.

The rise of big data capabilities is often critiqued from the standpoint of loss of privacy. But when technologies collect, catalog, and exploit data—much of which is willingly submitted by people—or when data is collected in open public spaces, then privacy is too narrow a concept to reflect what may be at risk.

What is actually at stake is the freedom to make the personal choices that affect our values and our destiny. A person can be manipulated and coerced in many ways, but the most ominous involve the pressure that comes with constant, ongoing surveillance of our actions. Our parents shape our behavior not only by teaching us as children, but also by the examples they set. They hope to instill strong value systems in their children even as they hope that their children will gain new opportunities, ideas, and experiences to mold them. As we grow older, we have more and more opportunities to choose our own way and explore new ideas.

But that freedom can be undermined when we lose control of information about ourselves—our actions, beliefs, relationships, and even our flaws and mistakes.

Modern analytic tools have the potential to form a detailed picture of almost any individual's activities. It is extremely difficult today to "opt out" of the data stream. Modern life generates data as a necessary part of the convenient services we enjoy. Information collected today is necessarily broader than what was collected in years past; it lasts longer; and it is put to more uses. But those who collect and aggregate that data have an increased power to influence and even coerce our behavior—possibly through social shaming and financial incentives and penalties.

Today's explosion of big data is often justified as promoting healthy lifestyles, convenient marketing, and even easier and more informed political engagement. But ubiquitous surveillance is a classic tool of oppression as epitomized by the Big Brother of George Orwell's *1984*, which watches constantly. Are we on the verge of inviting this oppression surveillance into our own lives, albeit in the deceptively benign guise of a "Big Nanny" who watches over us "for our own good"?

But the data explosion raises risks to more than our freedom. The expansion of online networks that are connected to physical systems, and that even control their operation, has dramatically expanded the ability of malign individuals to interfere with the physical world. This affects everything from generating the electricity that powers the grid to the performance of our automobiles. This expansion of network-controlled mechanical systems places an increasing burden on governments, private parties, and ordinary citizens to be able to secure their computers and systems against a surge of attacks from around the world. Traditional rules governing security and liability must adapt to and address these burgeoning threats. And this necessity to protect our world may conflict with the very real concern about the growing collection of our personal information.

One point should be clear. While it is customary to refer to modern big data developments as a result of the internet, that is an oversimplification. These developments were caused by changes in the way we collect, store, transmit, and analyze data, as well as in the interaction between digital transmissions and the operation of control systems that regulate our physical world. As I will describe, a confluence of circumstances drove these changes. Certainly, the creation of the internet was one, driven by the need for a flexible communications system that could survive natural or man-made destruction of the normal methods of communication. Other strides in data collection and analytics are the result of a new national security environment in which threats are no longer nation-states but instead online enemies who can be detected and thwarted only by monitoring the global movement of people, money, and communications. And even more profoundly, data has become valuable as a tool for targeted marketing and as a means of reducing the cost of executing commercial transactions. In short, the data revolution was powered by, and powered, the transformative expansion of our global economy.

Yet these revolutionary changes in the use of data have far outpaced our legal and policy architecture. We want to establish rules of the road to reconcile the competing demands for security, privacy, autonomy, economic growth, and convenience. But as security expert Bruce Schneier has observed, our legal system can be slow to adapt to technological change.[9] As I will outline here, we should not try to fit new technologies into the procrustean bed of existing outdated legal doctrines. What we need is to go back to basics: setting forth a clear understanding of the values we want to preserve, what challenges the world of big data presents, and how our legal system should evolve to address those challenges.

To put this effort in context, it's worth recalling that we have historically recognized the need to restructure our laws and policies when confronted with a technological disruption. We are actually in the third of three transformations in the history of surveillance and data (or information) collection. I call these periods Data 1.0, Data 2.0, and Data 3.0.

Data 1.0 refers to a time when information was collected prior to the invention of automated recording devices, such as cameras, telephones, and tape recorders. After writing was invented, records were limited to handwritten or printed notes or drawings. These were observations of what was seen or heard through face-to-face interaction, or what was read in another handwritten record. The reliability of this material depended upon the communicator's ability to mentally record and transmit it, either by telling someone else or by writing it down.

But the first transformation in the handling of data came with the invention of the printing press. This allowed broader dissemination of information and the ability to store writings in libraries. Even so, retention, dissemination, and usability of written information were restricted by limitations on storage space, reproduction, and modes of communication.

Data 2.0 refers to the time period after the invention of photography and telephony in the 19th century. Photographs allowed for superior recollection of events through reproduced images. Somewhat more comprehensive visual recording came with the arrival of video. Telephones enabled communication over longer distances more quickly. But telephones and microphones also allowed for deeper access into personal lives from remote locations via wiretaps and electronic surveillance devices, or "bugs." These technologies made life much more convenient, but at the same time they opened up new methods of surveillance. As I will explain, after a struggle, our laws governing these new data technologies need to evolve to strike a balance between these values.

Data 3.0 is today's increasingly digital world. Since the 21st century began, photographs are recorded no longer on film but in bytes of information that can be stored indefinitely, copied easily, and transmitted worldwide instantaneously on computers and smartphones and at will. As data storage memory systems improve, more and more data is captured and stored.

Data 3.0 is also characterized by the advent of data analytics—using computer software to examine vast troves of data, reaching conclusions that humans could not reach on their own. Mining data has provided many benefits, while it also enables pernicious uses. All this available data comes with societal consequences. We must learn to manage it in a way that protects individuals while enabling benefits to society as a whole.

And this is unlikely to be the last chapter in the evolution of how we handle data. We can imagine a Data 4.0—already prefigured with modern-day robots and artificial intelligence—in which embedded software in human beings creates true cyborgs: hybrid human machines. The initial steps toward this vision can be seen in the proliferation of wirelessly connected implanted medical devices like insulin pumps and pacemakers, as well as computer-driven limbs used to rehabilitate neurological or other medical deficits.

In thinking about how the law has evolved and should evolve, it's fundamental to clarify what values we want to preserve and rebalance. As I will describe later in this book, in the world of Data 1.0 the law primarily protected a privacy interest in physical spaces through property rights. At the time of the signing of the U.S. Constitution, the rule was that judicial permission was needed to search and seize in private physical space. When Data 2.0 arrived, technology like the telegraph and telephone shrank physical distances between spaces. The law adapted to protect a privacy interest in personal conversations, requiring a warrant to intercept conversations, even over publicly located telephone wires.

Today, Data 3.0 technology is again changing what is at stake. The sheer amount of personal data recorded, stored, and analyzed is staggering. New technologies have further blurred the line between what is public and what is private, and information once collected does not readily disappear. While we will always be concerned about our privacy in physical spaces and communications, the advent of mass collection, storage, analysis, and distribution of personal data means that we must also consider how we control data generated by or about us, even if it was not collected in what we might generally consider personal physical space.

What should we protect? Privacy is too narrow a value: it covers concealing only behavior that is sheltered from others in a private space or on privately designated communications facilities. In a world irreversibly governed by ubiquitous Data 3.0, hiding or obscuring behavior is impossible.

I argue that what we can and should care about is the broader value of *autonomy*, which is at the very core of freedom. Autonomy is the ability to make our own personal choices, restricted only by transparent laws and also influenced by social norms affecting our reputations within our communities. Autonomy is fundamental to human nature and respected in a modern, democratic society. Under the democratic ideal and the rule of law, citizens are bound only by law and regulations openly and democratically adopted and objectively enforced. Less coercively, our conduct is affected by norms honored within our own civil society institutions and communities.

These principles—the essence of the rule of law—are eroded when the availability of ubiquitous personal data means that any data holder (official or private) can use psychological manipulation, shaming, and financial incentives and penalties to influence and possibly coerce almost every facet of human behavior: what we watch, see, and eat; how we behave; and to whom we relate. When government has total access to your personal information, the practical reach of its authority is almost limitless, transgressing the formal constitutional or statutory limits on official power. Just as alarming, unfettered access to that data can allow private enterprises or groups to pressure, manipulate, or incentivize personal behavior without any public accountability. As is illustrated by the increasing phenomenon of online bullying, communities with which we have no connection can use data about us to retaliate or annoy us if they don't like our political or even aesthetic opinions.

To preserve space for lawful personal choice means that we must have significant control over data about ourselves—our likenesses, the things we do, our thought processes and decisions. A world in which every step we take factors into auto insurance or marketing, or allows the government to predict and regulate our behavior, would be a substantial constraint on our freedom of belief, our relationships, and our actions. Essentially, it means we would become programmed. We are moving in that direction.

We have always been worried that Big Brother might force his way into our home and compel obedience under his watchful eye. But Big Brother need not beat down the door. We are currently rolling out the red carpet to welcome him. And Big Brother is not just the government but also foreign nations, organized criminals, and even private companies. Indeed, as we incessantly record one another, we become Little Brothers and Sisters.

At a fundamental level, people should be aware of what is being done with their data, and they should make a choice about how to deal with it. Put another way, protection of our way of life must move beyond a right to conceal our data and into a broader right to control our data, even when hiding it or privately maintaining it becomes technologically impossible. Unless we take stock of our new digital environment and its consequences, we may lose not just privacy but also freedom and autonomy in the name of convenience.

CHAPTER ONE

WHAT IS THE INTERNET AND HOW DID IT CHANGE DATA?

Getting Connected

Methods for sending electronic messages have existed since the early 1800s in the form of the telegraph (the first "texting" machine!). Communications were passed by humans using Morse code to transmit electronic impulses over a wire connection. Over time, telegraphic machines were improved to allow for messages to be automated and sent worldwide. Then the telephone was invented, allowing oral conversation to be transmitted.

With the advent of the first practical telephone in 1876, a flurry of interest in expanding this convenient technology ensued. The American Telephone and Telegraph (AT&T) Company was incorporated in 1885.[1] Telephone service between New York and Chicago began in 1892.

Technological developments allowed for transcontinental telephone service in 1915.

The telephone system was based upon analog signals. This requires a variation of the electric signal to carry the voice reproduction as it is sent along a conductor. The original "networks" were completely owned by the telephone industry and comprised long connections of insulated copper wires strung out between population centers. Human operators made connections along the line. To make a phone call on this system, an uninterrupted connection had to be maintained between the caller and the person receiving the call, thus leading to the high price of making "long distance" phone calls.

The idea of sending a large amount of information, by breaking it into small "packets," was described by researchers in both the United States and the United Kingdom in the early 1960s.[2] This simple yet innovative idea was to break apart data into a digital format—blocks of "ones" and "zeroes," transforming words in a given message into "datagrams" that would be individually labeled to indicate the origin and destination of information, like individual data postcards. A constant connection between end points would no longer be required to send a large message. These datagrams could be sent electronically along any number of interconnected communications routes and assembled at the destination point after all had arrived.

In the late 1960s, the concept of using data packets was demonstrated on networks within closed research centers (with the first being created at the Lawrence Livermore National Laboratory, a nuclear weapons research center in

California). At the end of the 1960s, a relatively unknown government agency, the Advanced Research Projects Agency (ARPA), started researching methods for generically inter-connecting any computer network to another. ARPA's contracts sought to develop a generic system connecting academic computers between four places: the University of California at Los Angeles (UCLA), Stanford Research Institute (SRI), the University of California at Santa Barbara (UCSB), and the University of Utah. Because this had never before been accomplished, the challenge included both creating the system and the protocols that would allow for interlinking packet networks of various kinds. The system ARPA launched led to the establishment of networking standards for communication between computers.

The internet today continues to be based upon the relatively simple concept of breaking data apart into individual data packets (sets of ones and zeros), with a "label" indicating where they should go. These packets are then tossed into the "internet" and are passed around along one of many paths by devices called routers. They "read" the label and direct the packet on the shortest route to the intended destination. Once the message arrives at its intended destination, it waits to be reassembled into the data set or message.

Put another way: the message is broken down into small individually labeled and addressed data packets. This breaking up of information is done by the computer application creating the message (such as the web browser or the email program). The individual data packets are labeled with information to help them find a way out of the computer (which door or "port" to use) and the destination on the open network (a series of numbers that help point to the address on the internet).

The internet was designed to be neutral regarding the kind of data it was channeling. It could use any available path to send its packets along. If for some reason a route stopped working, the packets could move along a different one. The network simply passes the packets of data along to the desired destination. It is only upon reassembly of the data packets when they arrive at their destination that the conveyed information is meaningful. In an era when defense authorities were concerned about their ability to preserve communications lines in the event of a war, this element of multiple transmission pathways—the internet's resiliency—was a fundamental virtue.

The internet was also designed to be hardware independent. Any type of hardware could be used as long as it met the correct communication standards. The beauty in this architecture is that so many different types of computers can be connected to each other even with a variety of software and tools.

The internet is borderless. Data moves wherever pathways exist, without regard to legal boundaries or rules. As we will see, this feature disrupts customary legal constructs of sovereignty and jurisdiction.

To better understand how it operates, think of network communication on the internet in terms of the different steps it takes to send a message. The two most common ways of categorizing these steps are the Open Systems Interconnection (OSI) seven-layer model[3] and the Internet Engineering Task Force (IETF) four-layer model.[4] The

OSI model is actually more specific than the IETF model in defining what happens to data bits as they are processed and collected for shipping on the internet. But to help illustrate the process of sharing information on the internet, here is a brief description of the simpler four-layer IETF model, consisting of application, transport, internet, and link layers, along with the related physical layer.

Application Layer

Data created by all internet applications, or "apps," is first processed on the application layer. Here the content of any internet data assembled, sent, or received makes sense to people. Within the application layer, this data can be communicated to other apps on the same "host" or computer. The use of a web browser operating the Hypertext Transfer Protocol (HTTP)—the uniform system for maintaining addresses on the World Wide Web—is an example of the application layer.

At this layer, data bits are assembled and presented to the operator of the device. Here is where those bits become readable messages, viewable pictures and videos, or a visual presentation of your bank account balance.

Transport Layer

Within the transport layer, a channel for data exchange is created. Data is packaged for shipping within a local network (not on the "internet" per se, but within a locally managed network). Specific transport protocols (or standardized communication techniques) are used to begin communication, control the flow of data, and allow for data to be fragmented and sent over the broader internet, consisting of all networks connected by wire or wirelessly. The data is reassembled upon reception. These protocols address and send the data as messages within a local network.

Internet Layer

The internet layer is where data is sorted into different destinations. Communication between separate networks opens up through the use of internet addresses—technically Internet Protocol (IP) addresses. Think of them as precise zip codes for the internet that describe the destination of the data package.

The magic of routing enables the message to be sent toward its final destination. Routing can be thought of in terms of a traffic cop standing in the middle of an intersection. Unless a car is arriving at its final destination in that neighborhood, the cop is indifferent to the passing cars. The officer also has little regard as to the occupants of the vehicles. The cop's job is simply to keep traffic flowing in an organized fashion. The same can be said of the traffic controls at the internet layer. If at each intersection, or node, a message is trying to make its way through the internet, the local router's job is to pass it on to the next intersection with the expectation that it will eventually reach its intended destination and be flagged for collection by the traffic cop patrolling that intersection. The data packet may have to drive through multiple intersections in the internet to get there, but it is likely that it will eventually pass through its intended intersection and be pulled into the local network for processing toward the application layer.

Link Layer

The link layer ensures that data packets sent to it from the internet layer are passed along free of errors. This can be thought of as the clerk at the postal office. In order for a registered letter to be sent, the postal clerk ensures that the letter is correctly addressed, has a readable zip code, and is properly contained within the envelope. Prior to sending the datagram onward to the next data carrier on the internet, the link layer adds final shipping information to the data from the internet layer, along with data size information. Upon shipment toward its final destination, a timer is set to await confirmation of receipt.

Physical Layer

The physical layer is not an explicit element of the IETF four-layer system. But while people often describe the internet and cyberspace as "virtual," the internet does actually exist in physical space. It is obviously composed of an infrastructure of physical cables, connectors, routers, servers, etc., that are constantly evolving and expanding. Over time, the infrastructure has evolved to transmit more and more data at increasingly faster speeds. But this physical infrastructure remains the indispensable foundation on which the internet rests. Moreover, the location of key elements of the physical layer—servers, routers, cables, etc.—creates the possibility of controlling or even blocking the data that moves through that layer. Not surprisingly, therefore, control over the physical layer is often what nation-states focus on when seeking to assert control over globally mobile data.

Trust Was an Afterthought

A critical feature (or bug) of the original internet was that trust was an afterthought. This new system was not designed to be secure, because it did not need to be. The originators knew one another and trusted themselves to use the system for appropriate purposes. And because the number of users was initially very low, abuses could be easily rooted out and the offenders individually shamed into changing their behavior.

A by-product of this assumption of trust on the early internet was the casual approach taken to user identification. The ticket to admission on the internet, as an ecosystem, was nothing more than an end point with an IP address that could be linked to the network. While individual sites might require a password or another form of personal identification, the internet as a whole did not. As a consequence, any user could range freely over the internet, gaining access to any site not secured.

A system built on presumed trustworthiness has advantages and disadvantages. Because of its open and available architecture, the internet was able to develop very quickly. Connection could be done locally by any group desiring access. This was a stark contrast to the Ma Bell system, in which all the pieces of the network (including the telephone) were owned by the telephone company. Another advantage was that many different types of systems could easily communicate with one another. Messaging no longer depended upon a single end-to-end connection (like a transatlantic cable); rather, only one connection was necessary for the packets of data to be shared.

But there was a downside: trust can be exploited. In the mid-1980s, the first internet domain names were registered. These names used easy-to-remember text phrases to point at the underlying numbers that controlled the network addresses of computers. Until 1995, although formally under government control, all new domain names (such as google.com) were added free by the technical creators of the internet. As the system grew, so did the opportunity for it to be misused.

In 2004, John Zuccarini was sentenced to 30 months in prison for, among other things, using the domain name www .bobthebuilder.com to mislead children to a pornographic site.[5] This led the U.S. government to enact laws to try to ensure that domain names are neither false nor misleading.

Nor was the internet invulnerable to trickery. In 1988, a Cornell University student named Robert Tappan Morris launched a string of code that infected hundreds of computers across the internet. This so-called worm embedded itself in numerous computers by exploiting vulnerabilities in software and weak passwords. By running on a computer system, the worm would slow the machine's processing speed, especially if the system was infected multiple times. Hundreds of machines crashed and were rendered useless until they were disinfected. The Morris worm attack was merely a harbinger of the millions of denial-of-service, worm, and virus attacks that are now regularly reported around the world.

Going Wireless

Early internet communication required senders and recipients to enter the network by a telephonic link that connected into the infrastructure of wire or of cable, as does a landline telephone. The internet underwent a profound change with the expansion of wireless infrastructure. Communicators were now free from the physical limitations of wireline and no longer had a need to connect to a telephone or a similar fixed infrastructure.

Wireless access exponentially increased the number of end points that could be used to connect to a network and raised the prospect of mobile networks. Not only did this development allow users to access data on the internet from many locations, but, perhaps more important, it opened the possibility of devices autonomously generating data from virtually anyplace and sending that data to a network for storage and use. Here we glimpse Big Brother peeking out from behind a curtain.[6]

The ability to share information wirelessly was at first very novel. The capacity to take a laptop computer from the home office to the kitchen table and continue to be hooked up to the internet was convenient.

Telephone companies became determined to bring the internet to mobile telephones. Mobile phones were originally designed to allow for just a digitized voice and basic text data. Thus, the original digital cell phone networks, struggling to ensure nationwide voice connectivity, often lost connection. Competitors fought for customers by claiming to minimize the number of dropped calls.

The revolution began when mobile carriers designed networks allowing data to be disseminated more rapidly. Third-generation (3G) and then fourth-generation (4G) networks were created so that much more digital information could be shared. Networks increased data encoding and added multiple antenna paths to ensure that every consumer could reliably access fast digital data. Suddenly, the music you had been streaming on your PC at work or school could continue being streamed on your ride home. You could look up the website that you had just been viewing on your PC to satisfy your growing curiosity about what you'd just read. You could watch a streaming movie or look at your favorite social media site while waiting in the grocery store line. Not only could you pull up a map if you found yourself lost, but also your phone's GPS could guide you step-by-step to your destination.

The expansion of wireless access opened the door to making "dumb" devices into "smart" ones. Without any conscious act by an individual, phones, automobiles, appliances, and medical implants could be connected to send and receive data. This dramatically expanded the amount of data that could be harvested and, as we shall see, integrated and analyzed.

The increase in capability is penetrating the very fabric of society. In 2009, for the first time, network traffic for textual broadband data exceeded voice data on cellular networks.[7] During 2015, network traffic for 4G high-speed data exceeded that for 3G. Overall data traffic grew by 74 percent in 2015, by up to 3.7 exabytes per month.[8] (A typical computer hard drive today holds about one terabyte. One exabyte is one million terabytes. So, if you were to store all the traffic on mobile networks each month, you would need 3.7 million hard drives, all one terabyte each.)

Moore's Law

Not surprisingly, the huge expansion of data raised the question of what one might do with the data. This dovetailed with the growth of data storage capacity and chip storage capacity, allowing ever-increasing amounts of data to be held. Both these developments have transformed the internet from a method for communicating existing data among networks to a platform on which a public or private entity could exponentially increase the data collected from the physical world, processed, and stored for future reference.

The explosion in mobile devices added yet another layer of collections capability, including not only data generated by the device itself, but also pictures or communications that the device operator chose to input. For example, wireless connectivity with the internet created the ability to efficiently link a wide variety of physical sensors, like GPS devices, to cameras, license plate readers, and recorders of credit card and debit transactions.

The data explosion would have died in its infancy without the simultaneous explosion in data storage capacity. Some of this was an outgrowth of Moore's law: the observation by Gordon Moore, the cofounder of Intel, that the processing power per integrated circuit would be likely to double every two years. This doubling has led to the steady increase in storage capacity on individual chips. Just as important was the development of the "cloud," which is not literally an airborne repositioning of data. The cloud is actually a group of computer servers and software, interconnected as a means to efficiently store and process data from multiple sources.

The software allocates processing power and storage capacity to process data in the most efficient way. Without this dramatic increase in available processing storage capacity, there would have been a natural limit on the data one could or would want to collect. With virtually unlimited storage, all the "digital exhaust" generated by people interacting with collection devices can be captured and retained indefinitely at relatively low cost.

The rate of memory storage has roughly kept pace with Moore's law. The storage size of a computer hard drive itself has also doubled roughly every two years.[9] However, the cost of memory has decreased even more quickly. The price of a megabyte of storage has been halved every 14 months.[10] The first gigabyte-sized hard drive was introduced by IBM in 1980. It was the size of a refrigerator and cost $40,000.[11] As of the start of 2016, a terabyte-size hard drive could be purchased for about $50. In the past 35 years, we have become able to purchase 1,000 times more memory for 800,000 times less cost!

Capacious storage by itself would have little appeal without the ability to process and make use of this data. That requires the ability to identify, search, and interpret stored information faster than human analysis alone ever could. Data about location, financial transactions, and online activity would have little value in isolation, but when sorted and analyzed it yields a rich picture about users' preferences and activities.

The expansion of video monitors and feeds also led to the development of software tools to catalog, search, and correlate unstructured data, combining it with other information. These tools have allowed investigators, for example, to search events at a particular time and location by calling up a video record. But of even greater value is the ability to search a broad range of times and locations. This has spurred a demand for facial- and behavioral-recognition software that could search a large storehouse of video data to look for a particular person or type of behavior.

Ironically, the development of these analytic tools also increases the incentive for criminal behavior because the potential to abuse large amounts of data expands as well. For example, in 2015 it was revealed that millions of federal employee and applicant files stored by the U.S. Office of Personnel Management had been hacked and stolen. Some theorize that a nation-state sought these records to build a database for intelligence and counterintelligence purposes. What is clear, however, is that millions of stolen personnel files contain far too much data to be reviewed, retrieved, and categorized by unaided human beings. Thus, this trove of stolen files would be useless unless it could be efficiently sorted into categories, and its information extracted based upon characteristics of interest to the hacker. Increasingly sophisticated analytic capabilities, however, have made large databases of personal information more attractive as targets to hackers with criminal or espionage objectives.

Big Data's Possibilities

These developments in data collection, transmission, storage, and analysis are revolutionizing our economic and social behavior. Rapid and fundamental changes in data architecture have enabled the following activities to be executed online:

- Economic transactions
- Data collection, integration, storage, and availability
- Data analytics
- Direct control of physical control systems

Data-Driven Economy

According to the U.S. Census Bureau, e-commerce sales in the United States in 2016 were approximately $400 billion, almost 10 percent of all retail sales. In the financial sector,[12] online banking is a widely used service.[13] As of 2014, 87 percent of U.S. adults had cell phones, among which 61 percent were smartphones.[14] Surveys indicate that 51 percent of American adults bank online and that 32 percent bank using their mobile phones.[15] Mobile banking users can check their balances or recent transactions, transfer money, and deposit checks, all using their phones. In 2012, banking websites and mobile banking apps processed 2.5 billion bill-payment transactions.[16]

But beyond the number of transactions, the internet has fundamentally enabled the creation of new kinds of markets. By reducing transaction costs and expansion costs, the internet allows the rapid creation of new firms on a large scale; Amazon, Google, and Facebook are tech giants born only very recently. The internet also enables personalized goods and services; for instance, internet ads recommend products based on past purchases or browsing history. And the internet fosters rapid innovation—new products, payment systems, and pricing mechanisms grow quickly because companies run controlled experiments with online consumers and compare the results almost instantaneously.[17]

The sharing economy—loosely defined as peer-to-peer lending or collaborative consumption—helps people make use of excess capacity by renting out directly over the internet things like beds, cars, sporting equipment, formal wear, or pet sitting services.[18] Airbnb, which helps homeowners match spare rooms with travelers, averages 425,000 guests per night, or 155 million guest stays per year.[19] Uber, the ridesharing app, operates in hundreds of cities. Spotify, an online music platform, allows subscribers to listen to music without actually owning the track. From trading clothes to exchanging children's toys to renting out cars, Data 3.0 has changed our economic lives. At the same time, the peer-to-peer economy challenges traditional legal rules that regulate labor law or even antidiscrimination principles. For example, complaints have recently been raised that some homeowners on peer-to-peer lodging sites refuse to rent to minorities.[20]

Data 3.0 has also enabled efficient crowdsourcing. Wikipedia is one example—taking the ideas, time, and effort of people all over the world to develop and record knowledge. Through Kickstarter, 11 million people have supported initiatives from artists, musicians, and other creators, with $2.3 billion pledged and over 100,000 projects realized.[21] Even the IRS has launched a crowdsourcing challenge to come up with platforms that organize and present tax information for a better taxpayer experience.[22]

Data Everywhere

As the world has gone both digital and online, the amount of information automatically collected has become staggering. Retail giant Walmart handles more than one million customer transactions *every hour*.[23] Each of these is downloaded into databases of more than 2.5 petabytes (2,500 terabytes, or the size of about 2,500 typical hard drives).[24]

This expansion is driven by the fact that the creation and *storage* of data have been very low cost for data compilers. Because data compilers hope that this data could be later gleaned for nuggets of valuable information, it is rarely discarded. According to hard drive manufacturer Seagate Technology, the total amount of digital data generated in 2013 was about 3.5 zettabytes (3,500,000,000,000,000,000,000, or the ability to store the information on the equivalent of about 34 billion cell phones). By 2020, it estimates that we will be producing 44 zettabytes annually.[25]

Data Analytics

But, as noted previously, unusable data is garbage. It gets messier and more difficult to work with it unless it can be turned into something useful. As more and more data has been stored, new science in data analysis—including efficient methods for storing, searching, and analyzing information—has been developed. We are in the midst of a revolution in data analytics, in which the methods and tools for understanding large datasets and extracting useful information from them are emerging. Algorithms for intelligently analyzing data are constantly being invented and modified.

Data analytic tools are used for thousands of disparate purposes. Companies evaluate data to improve the debt collection process with self-learning algorithms that match up debtors and creditors in an online dialogue.[26] The decisions of business executives are being enhanced by data-driven results. A 2016 *Harvard Business Review* article called this the "cultural shift from 'Mad Men' to 'Math Men,'" in which decision making is increasingly based on data rather than on the frequently wrong opinions of senior executives."[27] Perhaps most significantly, data collection and analytics drive targeted advertising and marketing, for commercial enterprises as well as for political and ideological actors.

These new tools are not without their flaws and must be compared against known "truths" to be of real value. For example, the now shut-down "Google Flu Trends" website was long hailed as a shining example of the value of big data analysis. The website used data from individual Google searches to predict the state-by-state severity of annual flu cases.

However, these predictions were flawed, overestimating the cases of actual illness. They were more likely to have been "predicting winter, not flu."[28] Great care must be taken as we sift through digital exhaust to ensure that we do not jump to conclusions. Correlation may lead to suspicion, but it does not always equal causation.

Control of Physical Systems

The ability to control systems electronically has been available for decades. Programmable logic controllers (PLCs) are exactly what they sound like: devices that can be programmed to electronically control something else. PLCs open up valves in piping systems, enable and disable power switches, and run hydraulic systems and anything else that can be imagined for automation.

Supervisory control and data acquisition (SCADA) systems are a combination of electronic monitoring devices merged with PLCs. They are interconnected to run an entire system, like a factory or the power grid. These systems often control the various industrial manufacturing processes— water treatment plants; energy transmission systems; and heating, ventilation, and air-conditioning systems—that enable our modern lives. They ensure that the delicate balance between power production and delivery is maintained. They calibrate so that gasoline production plants keep pressure and flow rates within safe limits as well as at optimal output levels. As the internet has grown, so has the number of SCADA systems connected to it. This convenience allows engineers to manage and check on systems remotely.

But SCADA systems are vulnerable. They were never intended to be connected to a worldwide communications network. Instead, they were designed for closed environments, in which access was available only to on-site technicians. And, as previously observed, the internet was designed with the assumption that users were known and trusted. This means that the security of these systems is an afterthought. They are often easily hackable, not because they are poorly designed, but because they are being used outside their intended environment.

Moreover, the combination of dramatically expanding wireless bandwidth and increased processing power in computer chips places society at the threshold of a dramatic expansion of internet-controlled physical systems. The "internet of things" encompasses the ability to connect and direct almost any kind of mechanical system, whether it's automotive, medical, residential, or critical infrastructure. Household items like refrigerators, alarms, and thermostats are now being linked with one another, or remotely connected to a human or a computer. Regulating these various systems can be convenient and even economical, as in the case of the smart grid managing electricity usage.

But, as we shall see, insecure devices can create a broad surface area (i.e., many entry points) for destructive and even deadly online attacks.

The Deep Web and the Dark Web

The web is far from limited to what is readily searchable. The internet consists of not only searchable data but also a much larger volume of data accessible only to those who know its address or have access privileges. This is the so-called deep web, which cannot readily be searched using conventional search engines and can't be accessed through standard browsers. The deep web includes data from sites that are accessed only through application program interfaces, as well as instant messaging data and file sharing services. Also included in the deep web are private or academic databases. In some cases, the deep web includes data that search engines cannot index or cannot find, because they are password protected or require special software to access.

The deep web is vast. According to futurist Marc Good-man, Google is able to search and retrieve less than 1 percent of online information.[29] The deep web, according to some researchers, is 4,000 to 5,000 times larger than the surface web, and accounts for 90 percent of the traffic on the internet.

Much of the deep web is benign. This includes privately controlled sites operated by businesses or academic institutions, as well as some social media sites and file sharing services. But a small portion of the deep web is the so-called dark web, which can be accessed only through a special browser and is indexed through special sites not easily accessible and possibly requiring passwords. On the dark web, one may find a wide variety of illegal transactional activity. It takes advantage of the fact that much of the activity on the deep web occurs anonymously, using a special masking browser such as "the Onion Router," shortened to "Tor."

Tor was originally developed for very different purposes. The Naval Research Laboratory (NRL) developed it at the turn of the 21st century with the aim of providing anonymity to U.S. military personnel engaged in operations abroad.[30] The system makes it impossible to determine the IP address that originally requested a site. To ensure the anonymity of military users, the NRL deployed it in October 2003 as a free-to-the-public, open-source browser.[31] This meant that military traffic was hidden anonymously in a crowd of anonymous civilian users.

The mechanics behind Tor's anonymity are actually fairly simple. The system works by sending a site request through at least three randomly chosen computers, called relays.[32] Each computer adds to the signal a layer of encryption—like the layers of an onion—that only it can decrypt. The request then leaves a computer called the "exit relay," which is where the recipient perceives it to be originating from.[33] This makes users anonymous because exit relays might be making requests on behalf of hundreds of different users, and random algorithms determine what exit relay is used. About 7,000 volunteer computers world-wide serve as relays.[34]

It is important to note that the vast majority of Tor users are not accessing the dark web. They are using Tor to anonymously browse the surface web, often because they are located in a country that does not have free and open access to the internet. Tor users may also just be especially privacy-minded. Another large contingent of Tor users are performing deep web research.[35] Finally, some Tor users do access the dark web through the platform.

An early challenge for the dark web was that it was hard to find the hidden sites. The Hidden Wiki brought the first wave of users in 2004.[36] This site contains a catalog of all the dark websites that are currently operating, user feedback on those sites, and information about what can be accessed through each site. Another way to find sites is by using Tor-specific search engines such as Ahmia, which indexes any hidden sites it can find; and Grams, which specifically finds hidden sites selling illicit drugs, guns, and counterfeit money.[37]

To operate with better concealment, dark web market participants take advantage of so-called cryptocurrencies such as bitcoin, whose transactions are not tied to the banking system and allow for anonymity. Bitcoin's digital payment system, like that of other cryptocurrencies, relies on a publicly distributed and encrypted transaction ledger, known as the "blockchain," which facilitates bitcoin transactions while rewarding the owners of the computers that facilitate those transactions with newly issued bitcoin. The value of bitcoin varies with user demand.

An example of the dark web supporting a criminal eco system was Silk Road, an online marketplace for illegal goods and services. "The idea was to create a website where people could buy anything anonymously, with no trail whatsoever that could lead back to them," said Ross Ulbricht, arguably Silk Road's creator.[38] Known by his handle Dread Pirate Roberts, or simply DPR, Ulbricht managed a well-organized marketplace for illegal drugs and other illicit activities modeled on Amazon and eBay, with user profiles and product reviews. Categories of contraband and other offerings were listed, and correspondence between buyers and sellers was generally encrypted. From 2011 to 2013, Silk Road proved extremely successful—reaching some one million registered accounts and generating an estimated $1 billion in sales, with over 150,000 customers.[39]After nearly three years of trying to locate and unmask DPR, federal agents finally caught a break when DPR unwittingly revealed his IP address. Silk Road was shut down in October 2013, and Ulbricht was sentenced to life in prison without parole for money laundering, computer hacking, and conspiring to traffic illegal drugs. But Silk Road and other like websites reconstituted themselves, and different administrators took over.[40]

Since the FBI shutdown of Silk Road in October 2013, there has been an explosion in the dark web market for illegal goods. The market was previously centralized on Silk Road, but it has fragmented. A Reddit directory of dark web marketplaces is updated to inform users as to which are reputable and which are unreliable. The list of untrusted sites is far longer than the list of trusted ones.[41] Almost immediately after Silk Road was shut down, users flocked to a previously unknown site called the Sheep Marketplace. This site dominated the dark web market until a vendor exploited a vulnerability, stealing $6 million in bitcoin.[42] Former administrators of the original Silk Road launched Silk Road 2.0 on November 6, 2013, only one month after the original Silk Road was shut down. Silk Road 2.0 was short-lived. It was hacked in February 2014 by a vendor who stole $2.7 million in bitcoin.[43] That was not the end of Silk Road, however.

Silk Road 3.0, which has been operational since May 2016, is considered the most resilient dark net market.[44] While the U.S. government was involved with the takedown of the original Silk Road, it's clear the operation was not entirely successful. People quickly started up new dark web marketplaces. The government also failed to hold vendors or customers accountable for their transactions on the site.

The dark web continues to boom and increase its global reach. In 2017, law enforcement agencies in a dozen nations around the globe took down AlphaBay, which trafficked in all sorts of contraband and was called the largest dark net marketplace ever. Two hundred thousand users had millions of dollars in bitcoin held in AlphaBay accounts. In just two years, its ringleader had amassed a fortune of over $20 million.[45]

Cyber Crime, Terrorism, and Warfare

The internet has expanded unlawful opportunities for identity theft, credit card fraud, and outright theft of money. That's because online transactions often lack the indices of trust that we rely upon in the physical world. It seems that every day there is another news report of a giant hack; it's become commonplace for criminals to abscond with millions of credit card numbers and similar financial records, harvested from corporate and government databases. In 2015 alone, disclosed malicious exploits included the previously mentioned U.S. Office of Personnel Management intrusion, with the loss of 21 million individual records; the theft of data on 15 million T-Mobile customers through a hack into the network of Experian (ironically, a credit checking agency); the theft of password records from the password manager LastPass; and the potential intrusion into data of 80 million customers of health insurance company Anthem. In 2016, the Internet service provider Yahoo disclosed that an astonishing 500 million accounts had been compromised. In 2017, the U.S. Department of Justice charged two Russian intelligence agents, among others, with the Yahoo theft—demonstrating some state sponsorship of data theft. Also in 2017, Equifax, the credit agency, was forced to acknowledge the loss of data on 143 million Americans through a hacking episode.

Of course, data theft is just one way for criminals to monetize the subversion of internet security. Other methods include directly robbing banks. In 2013, international organized crime groups compromised two data companies in India that managed debit cards for multiple banks around the world. The group identified debit card numbers that could be used to withdraw unlimited amounts of cash from ATM machines. Having fabricated these cards, the criminal ring distributed them around the world and—in a single day—its confederates withdrew all the cash held by the target ATMs. One day's take? Forty-five million dollars.[46]

More recently, $81 million was stolen in an advanced attack on Bangladesh's central bank in February 2016. The hackers took advantage of the international electronic exchange network, called Society for Worldwide Interbank Financial Telecommunication (SWIFT), which was weakly controlled at its Bangladeshi connection point. The SWIFT system was not directly hacked, but the Bangladeshi bank's stolen credentials were used to issue fraudulent transfer orders.[47] These orders were actually "authenticated" by SWIFT, suggesting shrewd criminals who well knew the process.[48] A total of $951 million in fraudulent transfers was issued, although all but four requests[49] were eventually blocked.[50] (That still left the crooks $81 million.) The attack was timed to occur that so its discovery and a response would be delayed; the Federal Reserve Bank of New York couldn't reach the bankers in Bangladesh because their weekend had started. By the time the central bankers in Bangladesh discovered the fraud, the Fed's offices in New York had closed for the weekend.[51] The money was delivered to banks in the Philippines, and probably later to Filipino casino operators. The Philippines laws against money laundering do not apply to the gambling industry, so crime investigators were left with few options to further trace the disappearance of the money.[52] The cybersecurity firm Symantec has singled out North Korea as the culprit behind this cyber theft and others like it on banks in developing countries in Asia. If true, this would mark the first time a nation-state has used cyberattacks to steal money.[53]

Even extortion has gone online, with the dissemination of so-called ransomware. Criminals attack data held on a machine or network and encrypt it. They then send a message to the owner of this data, warning that if a blackmail payment is not made within a specified time, the decryption key will be destroyed and the data will be unrecoverable. The genius of the scheme lies in its scalability. The extortion payments requested—to be furnished with bitcoin, or some alternative financial mechanism—are usually relatively modest, so it becomes easier for victims to pay up than to report the episode to authorities, or to try to fight back. Because the internet allows these lawbreakers to attack thousands of machines, even modest individual ransom payments add up to major sums of money.

These ransomware extortion attacks have not just financial consequences but also effects on health and safety. The Hollywood Presbyterian Medical Center's network was hacked with ransomware that held its data hostage for several days. The hospital leadership acquiesced to the demands, paying about $17,000 in bitcoin to free their network from the ransomware.[54] In another hospital attack, this time against Methodist Hospital in western Kentucky, the administrators refused to pay to have the ransomware removed, but instead relied upon backups to get their systems back online.[55] It was fortunate they had backups, but waiting to see whether you can get the computers running again isn't always feasible in life-or-death scenarios. How quickly and how much would a hospital pay if its patients' automated heart pumps or medicine dispensers became infected with ransomware?

Indeed, ransomware has become viral. In 2017, the WannaCry exploit infected the U.K. National Health Service, a Spanish telephone system, and Chinese fuel stations, shutting down access to operational data. In total, 99 nations were affected by 75,000 separate attacks.[56] Almost immediately thereafter, a variant ransomware called NotPetya targeted key facilities in Ukraine, and incidentally crippled data access for Scandinavian shipping giant Maersk.

As damaging as data theft, fraud, and extortion can be, the potential for cyber criminals, terrorists, or nation-states to wreak real havoc lies in the relationship between networked data and its effects on the physical world. Physical control systems increasingly connect to data networks for monitoring and even directive purposes. The ability to gain remote entry to control systems has raised the risk that those systems can be compromised or damaged without someone needing physical access to the system itself.

For example, recent experiments have demonstrated that it is possible to seize control of an automobile through Bluetooth telephone connections, radio data systems, and cellular and Wi-Fi connections as used in various navigation and remote assistance services. Note also that voice-based embedded telephony could be hacked to remotely turn on the microphone and secretly record what occupants of a car are saying.[57] Other smart internet-connected machines that have been hacked include hotel room locks,[58] home alarms,[59] and even dishwashers.[60]

In 2013, Iranian hackers breached the computers controlling the Bowman Avenue Dam, a facility near the state border between New York and Connecticut, about 20 miles northeast of Central Park.[61] The 20-foot-tall dam itself is not particularly impressive. It is more of an environmental pond: a water-control dam that helps prevent flooding downstream by collecting rain runoff from the Blind Brook Creek. The 15-foot-wide, 2.5-foot-tall sluice gate controlling water outflow was automated in 2013 to help prevent flood damage as water levels change. The program controlling the gate was hacked via a cellular modem. This enabled hackers to gain control of the floodgates.[62] Fortunately, at the time of the hack, the sluice gate was under repair and offline, making any attempts to remotely manipulate it impossible.[63]

Some observers, such as the mayor of the small town where this dam is located, have suspected that the reason this particular dam was targeted was its name: it shares a name with another dam, the Arthur R. Bowman Dam on the Crooked River in Oregon, a much more impressive structure that is 245 feet tall and 800 feet long.[64] Perhaps, instead, the Iranians were attempting to breach this much larger facility? The consequences could have been much more severe.

Another cyberattack resulting in physical damage to infrastructure occurred in Ukraine in December 2015. This attack targeted three different electric power companies at approximately the same time, affecting 30 different electric power distribution facilities.[65] Legitimate access credentials were used, probably snatched through a targeted email containing malware (called phishing), to remotely log into the control computers and shut down the control switches. Operators watched dumbfounded as their cursors "skittered across the screen of [their] own accord," navigating to the appropriate shutdown applications, and clicking "yes" on the dialogue window that popped up to confirm the shutdown request.[66] A wiping utility, called KillDisk, then erased computer data, including the master boot record, preventing the electric companies from rebooting their computers after the breakers had been shut down.[67] Approximately 225,000 customers lost power for three hours.[68] When customers attempted to call their utility to report the outage, they could not get through. An attack on the phone system involving thousands of robocalls made at the same time, called a distributed denial-of-service (DDoS) attack, had commenced, with most of the calls coming from abroad.[69]

Fortunately, after just three hours, the electricity providers were able to restore power. Control operators drove to the affected distribution stations and manually restarted power with older legacy mechanical control switches.[70] However, according to the U.S. Department of Homeland Security, even two months after the attack, the power distribution companies "continue to run under constrained operations."[71]

By analyzing the cyber tools used in the attack (such as an access tool called BlackEnergy), the cybersecurity firm FireEye attributed it to the pro-Russian hacktivist group known as Sandworm.[72] Could an attack like this happen in the United States? Robert M. Lee, a former Air Force cyber warfare operations officer and now founder of a cybersecurity company, helped investigate the event at the request of the U.S. government. He said, "Despite what's been said by officials in the media, every bit of this is doable in the US grid [though] the impact would have been different and we do have a more hardened grid than Ukraine."[73] The United States has a much more automated system than Ukraine, so if an attack were to occur, restoration may not be as simple as driving to a remote substation and flipping on a breaker. The Department of Homeland Security has recently warned U.S. industrial firms of a hacking campaign targeting nuclear and energy sectors.[74]

The data revolution has transformed economics, commerce, society, physical systems, and opportunities for crime and terrorism. Imprudently, the policy and legal framework regulating these areas has not kept pace with these changes. Too often, policy discussions of how to manage and regulate data are trapped in a sterile debate of trade-offs between convenience, security, and privacy—applying stale 20th-century concepts about each of these domains. The history of legal developments has, however, demonstrated that technological revolutions can beget legal revolutions. We are primed and overdue for the next one.

CHAPTER TWO

HOW DID LAW AND POLICY EVOLVE TO ADDRESS DATA 1.0 AND 2.0?

The legal and policy architecture of privacy and data absolutely must evolve to meet the challenges of Data 3.0. Before we explore how we might accomplish that, it is useful to look back at the past technological inflection points of Data 1.0 and 2.0, when indeed law and policy were reformulated.

Data 1.0: Trespass

In November 1762, four agents of the British Crown broke into the home of John Entick in the Stepney neighborhood outside London. Entick was a pamphleteer, writer, and critic of the government. Over the next four hours, these men, acting under the authority of senior government officials, sought evidence of seditious and disloyal writings. The agents rifled through cupboards and drawers, seizing and removing hundreds of papers and causing a great deal of physical damage. Entick sued the agents for trespass, and the English Court of Common Pleas upheld the suit, ruling that the physical intrusion into and seizure of papers from Entick's home, without a clear basis on legal authority, was not legal.[1] Deemed "on[e] of the landmarks of English liberty,"[2] Entick's case informed the U.S. Constitution when its framers drafted the Fourth Amendment prohibiting unreasonable and overly general searches and seizures.[3]

One year earlier, in 1761, a similar case arose in colonial Massachusetts. Seeking to clamp down on colonial merchants suspected of smuggling goods into Boston, British customs officials sought "writs of assistance" allowing them to search—without probable cause or individualized suspicion—private homes and businesses and to seek the assistance of subjects in conducting these raids.[4] Lawyer James Otis represented a group of merchants challenging the writs as unlawful and a warrantless invasion of privacy. Although Otis lost, the case helped spur the American Revolution. John Adams wrote about Otis's argument, "Then and there was the child Independence born."[5]

By adopting the Fourth Amendment to the federal Constitution, the newly born United States sought to protect its citizenry from unreasonable searches and seizures; states adopted similar provisions in their constitutions. But at the time of the adoption of the American Bill of Rights, and during the first century after the country's independence, personal data meant what was seen, heard, and written down. Indeed, by its terms the Fourth Amendment protects "the right of the people to be secure in their persons, houses, papers, and effects, against unreasonable searches and seizures."[6] Privacy issues, therefore, were primarily a function of property rights in physical spaces. The law developed around search warrants for *physical* intrusions or seizure of *physical* items like documents. This was encapsulated in the shorthand formula that a citizen's home "is his castle," which connotes a physical fortress. After the framing of the U.S. Constitution, American courts generally based privacy protections on a finding of an invasion into private property or the uninvited touching of a physical person.

Data 2.0: Misappropriation Theory

In the late 19th and early 20th centuries, the law faced the development of new technology for recording visually and aurally. Use of photography led to instances where people photographed in public places had their images appropriated for commercial purposes. Also, technological developments in printing and publication allowed words and images to be more widely disseminated than in the past. Since the photographer was a third party, and provided there was no physical trespass onto the property of the photographic subject, what restraint if any could be imposed on use of an image taken in public?

In 1900, Abigail Roberson, a young woman of 18 living in Rochester, New York, had photographs taken at a portrait studio. She gave them to her boyfriend, who told her that an artist friend was going to use them to create a portrait. In fact, without her consent the young man sold the pictures to a local flour mill company for commercial use.[7] The company used her likeness on some 25,000 prints and photographs in flyers and magazine advertisements, with the phrase "Flour of the Family." Roberson complained that local residents recognized her likeness—although the photographic image actually appears to have been oblique—and made her "greatly humiliated by the scoffs and jeers."[8]

Roberson sued, claiming the unauthorized use of her likeness and invasion of her rights caused her "nervous shock" and mental distress.[9] She claimed she was bedridden and had to hire a physician. Perhaps more significantly, Roberson was not compensated for the commercial use of her image. She wanted $15,000 in damages and a court order to halt the printing of her likeness.[10]

The lawsuit worked its way up to the highest court of New York. In a narrowly divided decision, the state saw no injury to a protectable privacy interest when there was commercial appropriation of a photographic image provided there was no accompanying defamatory falsehood (analyzed as a separate form of injury to one's interest or reputation). In *Roberson v. Rochester Folding Box Co.*, the majority of the court rejected her claim. The court acknowledged that the law protects against false and defamatory use of an image, or the use of a photograph that represented a breach of trust or a theft of property (if a photograph were stolen, for example). But Roberson's basic interest in maintaining control over her likeness was considered too insubstantial to deserve protection.[11] In short, the purely "mental character of the injury" did not persuade the court to grant Roberson compensation.[12] The decision generated a public outcry, and the New York State legislature soon after enacted a statute protecting the right to privacy. It remains on the books to this day.[13]

Three years after *Roberson*, the supreme court of Georgia considered a similar lawsuit, arising from the unauthorized use of a photo in an insurance advertisement, together with the false claim that the plaintiff was a policyholder. This time, the court ruled that there had been a breach of the plaintiff's privacy. It reasoned that the unauthorized appropriation and commercial use of one's likeness and identity amounted to an infringement of liberty because the subject was "for the time being under the control of another" and "no longer free."[14]

This decision, and others that followed, echoed a seminal law review article from 1890 that questioned whether the surge in press coverage about the details of individual scandal and personal behavior warranted the protection of a person's "right to be let alone."[15] The authors, future justice Louis D. Brandeis and Samuel D. Warren, pointed to existing legal protection for property and reputations, and extrapolated a broader theory of protecting individuals against public dissemination of information about their private life. Again, the impetus for this proposed protection of "private facts"—that is, facts not of general public interest or not involving a public figure—was the technological advances of photography and mass-market publishing that dramatically increased what might be disseminated in the press or elsewhere about an ordinary person, even assuming there was no trespass on property or no actual falsehood.

Brandeis and Warren articulated the existence of a human interest in protecting details of private life, even if true, against widespread public distribution and observation. As they put it, "to occupy the indolent, column upon column is filled with idle gossip, which can only be procured by intrusion upon the domestic circle."[16]

Subsequent common-law cases and legal scholars ultimately recognized limited protection against public disclosure of private facts or the unauthorized use of someone's identity or likeness for commercial purposes. While the precise interest being protected is still the subject of debate, the expanded right to privacy steps outside the concept of physical property. This legal evolution gave average citizens a measure of control over their personal dignity, the power to define their identity, and the right to exclusive control over the commercial exploitation of their name and likeness. These, of course, are elements of our society's broader interest in autonomy.

Data 2.0: Wiretapping

Another episode that reordered the concept of privacy in response to technological change was the development of wiretapping and electronic surveillance. The illegality of eavesdropping—seeking to overhear what is being spoken in a private location—was rooted in the property interest against physical intrusion into a house or telephone line. The ability to eavesdrop efficiently was limited before the 20th century; the eavesdropper had to gain access to the location and the speakers and be sufficiently close to overhear any conversation. This was likely to mean physical trespass, illegal without a warrant.

Telephony altered this. As telephone lines passed outside individual homes and into public space (or the telephone company housing the switches), it became technically possible for the curious to intercept phone conversations while away from the speakers, and without physically trespassing on private property. Other technological developments soon allowed for recording face-to-face conversations, if a microphone could be placed in physical proximity to the speakers.

Initially, the courts responded to telephone wiretapping by adhering to the physical-property-based theory of privacy for conversations. The interest to be protected was not speech between two or more people; it was the sanctity of the physical space where that speech took place.

Consider Roy Olmstead, who ran a major Prohibition-era bootlegging operation in Seattle that used boats and trucks to illegally smuggle alcohol into the United States from Canada.[17] His operation allowed customers the convenience of placing liquor orders by phone. At its height, Olmstead's business delivered over 200 cases of liquor daily to Seattle hotels, restaurants, and homes. A former police officer, Olmstead bribed the sheriff and local police to keep his business running and became known as "King of the Northwest Bootleggers."[18] Beginning in June 1924, however, federal agents tapped the telephone wires extending from Olmstead's house without trespassing on private property. The agents listened to his calls for months, producing over 700 pages of transcripts. The conversations alone did not yield sufficient evidence to charge Olmstead, in part because he knew about the wiretaps. (So thoroughly had Olmstead bribed the authorities that the agent in charge of wiretapping offered to sell him the transcripts!)[19] However, Canadian authorities later seized from Olmstead's gang a boatload of liquor bound for the United States. The Canadian testimony, in combination with the information gleaned from the wiretaps, allowed federal agents to obtain a warrant to search Olmstead's operation. The combined evidence led a grand jury to indict Olmstead and 90 others for conspiracy to violate the National Prohibition Act (also known as the Volstead Act). Olmstead was sentenced to four years in prison and had to pay $8,000 in fines.[20]

The case made its way to the U.S. Supreme Court. In *Olmstead v. United States*, the court narrowly rejected Roy Olmstead's challenge to warrantless police wiretapping of external telephone lines on the grounds that the telephone user—Olmstead—knew that his voice would travel into a public space along phone lines, and the constitutional privacy protections of the Fourth Amendment extended only to a "man's house, his person, his papers, and his effects, and to prevent their seizure against his will."[21]

Olmstead provoked vigorous dissents from four justices. Justice Brandeis observed that Fourth Amendment principles must adapt to address technological innovation, presciently noting that the "progress of science in furnishing the government with means of espionage is not likely to stop with wiretapping."[22] By the time of the Court's decision, popular will had been felt through legislative policymaking: 41 of 48 states had put into law limits on warrantless wiretapping. Congress soon passed a similar restriction on wiretapping but did not address eavesdropping with a microphone in a physical space.[23]

The law of eavesdropping developed along a similar course. As the technology for recording in physical spaces developed, the Supreme Court first made the key to individual protection whether or not a recording device physically intruded into private property. Over time, the justices signaled that the interest to be protected might center not on private physical space, but rather on the expectation of confidentiality that existed between speakers. In other words, the Fourth Amendment should not only protect property from intrusion, but also protect the speakers' ability to control how their speech should be directed.

In the 1960s, Charles Katz was a leading "handicapper" for college basketball. He made a living by placing bets for gamblers and taking a cut of the winnings for himself.[24] Federal law prohibited interstate gambling, so to escape detection Katz regularly walked from his apartment on Sunset Boulevard in Los Angeles to a set of three public telephone booths. From there he placed long-distance calls to Boston and Miami, using coded language to mask the gambling. When FBI agents learned of Katz's activities, they developed an elaborate plan to catch him. The agents first got the telephone company to label one booth "out of order." They then placed a microphone and recorder on top of and between the other two telephone booths. Finally, an agent stationed near Katz's apartment would signal when Katz left his home, and another agent would then quickly turn on the recording devices. The FBI successfully recorded Katz's conversations over several days and proceeded to prosecute him.[25]

Although the FBI did not have a warrant to record Katz's conversations, under *Olmstead* it did not need one, because there was no physical trespass. Recall that in *Olmstead* the Supreme Court had found no warrant was required when federal agents had wiretapped the phone lines extending from Olmstead's home. Indeed, when the Supreme Court heard *Olmstead*, many neighbors shared "party" telephone lines on which they had no expectation of privacy.

The FBI had recorded Katz's conversations from a public telephone booth. The government argued that Katz had no expectation of privacy in a public phone booth with a glass door. By 1967, however, the Supreme Court was prepared to recognize a right to privacy in oral communications.[26]

In *Katz v. United States*, the Court rejected *Olmstead* and explicitly ruled that the Fourth Amendment protects "people, not places."[27] Analysis should focus not on the character of a physical space but on the intent of an individual to preserve confidentiality of certain communications. Evidence from the FBI's recordings was suppressed and Katz's conviction overturned.

In the *Katz* judgment, technological evolution redefined what constitutes behavior deserving of privacy protection. If you speak in a physical setting or on a physical device closed to the general public, you have a right to protect that data, even if there is no physical intrusion into your property. Wiretapping is therefore permitted only with a judicial warrant. On the other hand, if you speak within open hearing of others in a public area, you have not reasonably signaled an intent to maintain confidentiality and you have no right to protect what you have said. This gives rise to the third-party doctrine: if you convey data to a third party, like a communications service provider, your privacy protections are much diminished.

In *Katz*, technological changes resulted in a redetermination of our society's limits on government surveillance and investigation. The courts refocused legal protection away from physical space and onto the interest in confidentiality in communications. But by formulating these new legal protections in terms of the individual's "expectation of privacy" the courts embedded public opinion in the definition of those protections. And that proved to be a weakness when the next data revolution began to modify social expectations.

What Is Public? How Society's Expectations of Privacy Evolved

In the early 1900s, what was meant by public activity was fairly obvious: conversation or information not maintained in a private space, and therefore expected to be visible or audible to others. But where communications occurred in a private space, Americans expected to have a reasonable amount of protection for that privacy. This could be invaded only under justified, warranted intrusion by the government.

As the telephone moved from an exclusive convenience of the wealthy and became adopted by all, the desire increased to tap into these communications to aid in capturing criminals. During World War I, wiretapping became so commonplace that Congress outlawed the practice—despite the obvious threats to national security posed by spies and saboteurs.[28]

Recall that during the Prohibition era, the Supreme Court found in a 5–4 verdict that the wiretaps placed on bootlegger Olmstead's phones did not require a warrant. However, when the case was considered in a lower court— the Ninth Circuit Court of Appeals—one judge would have imposed a warrant requirement even without a physical trespass. In a dissenting opinion, Judge Frank Rudkin argued, "A person using the telegraph or telephone is not broadcasting to the world. His conversation is sealed from the public as completely as the nature of the instrumentalities employed will permit, and no federal officer or federal agent has a right to take his message from the wires, in order that it may be used against him. . . . If ills such as these must be borne, our forefathers signally failed in their desire to ordain and establish government to secure the blessings of liberty to themselves and their posterity."[29] Although wiretapping was not ruled illegal in the 1930s, public opinion was increasingly against it. That sentiment was finally reflected in the 1934 Communications Act, which for the first time made it illegal to tap telephones and disseminate the content of what was overheard.

But as the threats to national security rose, the public arguments for wiretapping and eavesdropping became more compelling. When the world was being swept into the chaos of World War II, President Franklin Roosevelt wrote a memo to Attorney General Robert Jackson on May 21, 1940. In it, FDR "authorized the necessary investigat[ing] agents that they are at liberty to secure information by listening devices ... of persons suspected of subversive activities ... including suspected spies."[30] Secured in a time of great fear and for the public good, these new powers were then used by the government to investigate anyone thought "subversive." Throughout the war, wiretapping continued. After it, in the 1950s, a fear of communism drove "McCarthyism" to expand the use of wiretaps.

On March 30, 1949, a 27-year-old political analyst for the Justice Department, Judith Coplon, was charged with espionage after she was arrested on a Manhattan street corner with Soviet agent Valentin A. Gubitchev. After a tip-off from an intercepted Soviet cable, Coplon had been snared in a sting operation that involved passing her a falsified memo about atomic power and tracking her movements. The leaked memo, along with several other secret documents, was confiscated from her possession. She was convicted; however, when the FBI disclosed that it had obtained evidence against her through wiretapped conversations illegal under the 1934 Communications Act, including some with her lawyer, the appeals court overturned her conviction.[31] Coplon later married one of her lawyers, a decorated WWII veteran, and ran restaurants in Manhattan before dying at the age of 89 in 2011.

Even as the Supreme Court's 1967 decision in *Katz v. United States* ruled that the Fourth Amendment protections against unreasonable searches extended to telephone conversations, the legal evolution in balancing individual privacy and evolving security needs was slow to progress. The 1968 Omnibus Crime Control and Safe Streets Act took a first step. It accepted *Katz* and clarified that while wiretapping was covered by the Fourth Amendment, the government could obtain a warrant as required by that amendment to wiretap an individual to investigate specific crimes, such as murder, kidnapping, and organized crime.[32]

Counterintelligence activities undertaken in support of national security and defense presented other issues. In the 1970s, the United States was deeply entrenched in the Cold War with the Soviet Union. The primary national concern was the nuclear threat, and spying was deemed to be one of the most effective ways to quell this problem. Counterintelligence agents were given significant flexibility in tracking down foreign adversaries. The legal issues arose when foreign spies approached Americans for recruitment, creating a "gray area" for intelligence investigators. At that point, the line between collecting intelligence on foreigners and collecting it on Americans began to blur, for Americans might be acting as foreign agents.

In 1973, following the Nixon Watergate scandal, CIA director James R. Schlesinger commissioned a set of reports, now informally called the CIA's "Family Jewels," outlining CIA counterespionage activities that may have fallen outside the agency's legal authority.[33] Some of the content of these reports was revealed by the *New York Times* in a front-page article on December 22, 1974, that stated, "The Central Intelligence Agency, directly violating its charter, conducted a massive, illegal domestic intelligence operation during the Nixon Administration against the antiwar movement and other dissident groups in the United States. . . . Intelligence files on at least 10,000 American citizens were maintained by a special unit of the C.I.A."[34]

The allegations by the *New York Times* sparked a congressional investigation and the eventual establishment of a new court system with the Foreign Intelligence Surveillance Act (FISA) of 1978. The FISA courts were charged with "oversight of foreign intelligence surveillance activities while maintaining the secrecy necessary to effectively monitor national security threats."[35]

The USA PATRIOT Act and Surveillance Reform at the Birth of the Internet Age

Most communications during the early 1980s were done on traditional analog phone lines. As the internet evolved to include digitized communications such as wire transfers, electronic mail, and digital voice calls, new avenues of surveillance opened up.

Although wiretaps on domestic phone lines were illegal, it could be argued that it was completely legal to intercept digital data communications on the internet because *Katz* and the laws passed by Congress dealt only with telephone technology. Therefore no explicit laws had been passed to prevent interception of internet communications.[36] Unlike a closed point-to-point communications system such as wireline telephony, communications over the internet travel through an infrastructure open (in theory) to anybody. To remedy this technological gap in the law, Congress passed the Electronic Communications Privacy Act of 1986, requiring that electronic communications have the same legal protections as phone communications, though conversations made on cordless phones were not protected.[37] This also established rules for the use of pen registers (devices that record the numbers dialed out from a phone) and trap-and-trace devices (systems that record the numbers coming into a specific phone). After passage of the law, the Senate report commented:

> The law must advance with the technology to ensure the continued vitality of the fourth amendment. Privacy cannot be left to depend solely on physical protection, or it will gradually erode as technology advances. Congress must act to protect the privacy of our citizens. If we do not, we will promote the gradual erosion of this precious right.[38]

Not surprisingly, the next notable changes in surveillance and security requirements came in the wake of the traumatic attacks suffered on September 11, 2001. Those, including me, who steered the Department of Justice's immediate response, realized we needed to recalibrate our intelligence collection. The ability of al Qaeda terrorists to enter the country and a concern about follow-up attacks placed a premium on harvesting large volumes of data about travelers to get early warnings about terror operatives. New demands transformed intelligence gathering from traditional espionage targeting foreign leaders and officials to the more difficult effort to find a terrorist needle hidden in the haystack of a civilian population.

A flurry of legislation, including the USA PATRIOT Act, enabled the government to expand its ability to collect and review data. The new law sought to synchronize authorities collecting information over the internet with the existent authorities' collection of telephony and analog communications. But a gray area was what privacy restrictions should be applied to the collection of communications originating or ending overseas (for example, a suspected Syrian terrorist phoning his cousin living in the United States). Was this domestic communications interception governed by FISA, or could it be deemed part of the essentially unrestricted espionage activities conducted by U.S. intelligence in foreign countries? The U.S. government initially took the latter position, but after a few years Justice Department attorneys balked, refusing to approve this warrantless surveillance. The result was a new statutory scheme that did not require a warrant for surveillance directed at overseas non-American targets but did require the FISA court to supervise the collection process to ensure that the government was not circumventing the warrant requirement where U.S. residents were being targeted.

Under the 2008 FISA Amendments Act, therefore, the executive branch may target non-U.S. persons outside the United States (or believed to be) for warrantless electronic surveillance. While judicial review is not required in individual cases, the courts are mandated to periodically review targeting procedures in general. They want to make sure information-gathering efforts are reasonably tailored to avoid surveilling Americans or others physically within the United States. On the other hand, the government must obtain a warrant to legally surveil a U.S. person or a foreigner within the United States. The balance struck is to be very protective of the privacy rights of U.S. citizens and those within our borders, but less so of foreigners overseas.

But even those restrictions do not apply to a type of electronic information gathering that became increasingly important in the post-9/11 world. It was no longer just important to intercept actual conversations or text communications between terrorists. Now so-called metadata could be effectively used to map potential links and connections from known terrorists to unknown members of their network. Metadata is essentially internet or telephonic addresses and routing instructions (or financial routing instructions) that identify who is communicating with whom (or whether two people are engaged in a financial transaction). It may be compared to the address information on the outside of a sealed postal envelope. While this information is not private in the classic sense—it does not reveal the actual content of a conversation—it reveals something about one's affinity group. In bulk, this information can be reasonably instructive about someone's social behavior.

Both before and after 9/11, the collection of metadata was deemed to require only a modest legal protection of privacy: merely a show of relevance to a criminal or national security investigation.[39] But because of the dramatic increase in internet communication and data storage over the preceding decade, it became feasible and appealing for the first time to have the government collect and hold metadata of all communications to conduct analysis on a massive scale. Although review of specific data required some predicate showing of reasonable basis, the maintenance of the database allowed almost any tangible lead to be pursued. It allowed identification of even remote links from known terrorists to others.

For a number of years, metadata collection was a valuable tool in the U.S. counterterror arsenal as a means to flag potential unknown terrorists. But when the enormous scale of information collected became public, partly because of the extensive theft of data by Edward Snowden, a negative reaction occurred. Even though only minimal data was collected about any single individual, the fact that almost all Americans had metadata collected under the program made it seem larger in scope and more alarming than anything previous. In 2015, the USA FREEDOM Act ended this bulk collection of all metadata by the National Security Agency (NSA), requiring that in the future the government leave metadata within the databases of individual telecommunications companies and service providers, to the extent they maintain that information. Any searching of that metadata would require some specific relevance.

These modifications of the legal landscape reflect the contemporary evolution of expectations of privacy, and at the same time influence and alter those expectations. This feature of the legal evolution exposed the conceptual flaw in *Katz*: building a privacy rule around "expectations" was circular reasoning because the rule itself shaped or reshaped expectations. If legal rules allow greater latitude for surveillance, expectations themselves might degrade, pointing toward even greater surveillance. If surveillance restrictions are tightened, expectations arguably increase, leading to further constraints.

That circularity to the *Katz* formula intensifies in the face of the technological revolution of big data. As we will see, given the ease with which emails, telephone metadata, and other forms of previously private information are captured by many private—let alone government—enterprises, Americans have become accustomed to surrendering control over electronic privacy. We have adjusted our expectations to a world in which our data is being routinely collected and used by others. Can expectations still be the touchstone of what is permitted when the private sector collects vast data emanating from devices that record what we read, where we go, what we buy, and even our biological characteristics? Today's legal framework attempts to protect the right to privacy under a technology assumption that is decades old.

At the same time, new internet technologies create unprecedented threats to our individual safety and security. An outmoded legal framework not only undervalues protections against the government's abuse of data collection and analysis but, conversely, inadequately protects that data and those networks against external threats from criminals, terrorists, and even nations.

With the expectation that the existing social norms and laws still apply, we have attempted to merge new technologies into an existing legal structure. However, with new technology drastically changing our expectations about what "private" and "public" mean, we must now determine what social values and principles need to be safeguarded. The broader concept of autonomy—the right to control data about ourselves, and thereby shape our own destiny—is at the core of what must be protected.

CHAPTER THREE

DATA 3.0 AND THE CHALLENGES OF PRIVACY AND SECURITY

The World Wide Web is a network of networks in which tremendous volumes of data are stored online and—absent specific protective measures—can be accessed by anyone who can get online. The dramatic expansion of data collected, how easily it is transmitted, how long it is stored, and how efficiently it can be aggregated and analyzed have huge social implications—much more profound than those generated by the emergence of photography and telephony. Compounding the revolutionary changes is today's extensive use of mobile devices and of wireless technologies, which offer a much greater outward-facing surface area through which a network can be operated—or penetrated.

The new data revolution has fundamentally altered the conceptual distinction between private and public information. Under the data structure that existed before the 21st century, data or information about an individual was relatively easily divided into nonpublic (private discussion, activity in private space, discussion on a telephone between two or several defined people) and public (activity ordinarily visible to the public, such as that on the street or at a window, and discussion audible to an undefined group of people in the street, etc.). But the current architecture of data collection, storage, and use blurs the distinction between what is private and what is obviously public.

One aspect of this blurring is the increasing unrestricted collection of data as the embedded price of various "free" online services. For example, *Angry Birds* is the tremendously popular game for mobile phones that slings birds toward piggies to eradicate them. It can be downloaded free and has been downloaded more than a billion times. However, most people don't stop to ask the question, "How are the developers getting paid for this application?" In the case of *Angry Birds*, most users—who don't read the application's disclosure policy—don't realize their data, such as location, unique cell phone ID number, or gender is being collected, packaged, and transferred to so-called advertising partners.[1]

Data about individual users has become a lucrative commodity. It is now a multibillion-dollar industry that operates in the legal gray area surrounding the internet.[2] If you didn't know the app on your phone is collecting data, is that okay as long as you enjoy the other benefits (such as playing *Angry Birds*)? Does it matter that the data collection facts were buried in an endlessly long consent form that you failed to read while installing the application? At what point does this data collection become invasive—When your name is collected? Or your contact list?

Surveillance laws were written to protect against wire-tapping on private phone lines and eavesdropping in closed spaces by anyone except agents with a warrant. But now people regularly, and often unknowingly, leak data where it can be picked up and reviewed by others. And this avail-ability of your data is not confined to the provider of any specific online service. Given legal authority, government officials may view the data. This information about you may also be purchased from the provider. Or it might be seen and collected by those who hack into the provider and steal the data. This data does not decompose and can later be assembled into an ever more complete picture of your daily activities. Obviously, the context in which we view historical protections for "private" and "public" information needs to be updated.

"Public" Means So Much More Today Than It Used to Mean

Until quite recently, acts or statements performed in public were by definition fragmentary: they had inherent limita-tions regarding how widely they could be disseminated, how broadly they could be aggregated, and how long they would persist. Unless individuals were under constant surveillance or being relentlessly stalked, it was well-nigh impossible to collect all their statements or acts, even those occurring in public. Most utterances and behavior in public places were unrecorded, and even if they were recorded or photographed there was no means to aggregate them. Furthermore, whatever data could be collected and recorded was difficult to disseminate widely. Over time, much would be lost to memory because of physical and financial limits on the ability to store information indefinitely. Thus, the collection, distribution, and storage of an individual's statements and acts—even those occurring in the wide-open public space—necessarily degraded or were lost over time. This characteristic I call *information friction*. Importantly, information friction essentially ameliorated the adverse consequences of a public act by reducing the practical possibility that it would be connected with other acts, that it would be stored indefinitely, and that it would be widely published. In short, we could forget and—except in extraordinary cases—we could count on the forgetfulness of others.

But under the Data 3.0 architecture of the 21st century, the characteristics of both private and public behavior have changed. Any data or information connected to the internet—even if entered and maintained in an apparently private space, like a home or business computer—is structurally accessible to anyone else in the world with access to the internet *unless* the creator or possessor of the information has affirmatively taken steps to protect it. In other words, the *default setting* for such information has changed from private to public with indefinite retention.

Similarly, the nature of what happens to data generated in public has changed. It is now relatively easy to collect and aggregate all of an individual's public acts. The explosion in video and audio technologies, especially on individual smartphones and other mobile devices, as well as ubiquitous cameras and license plate readers in major cities, means that many more public acts are recorded, especially acts by individuals. Similarly, the expansion of social media and easy-to-use tools means that people frequently post comments about behavior they have observed or experienced in near real-time.

Video and Audio Surveillance Is Everywhere

We now find ourselves in a world in which video recording of our behavior is simple and pervasive. More mobile phones exist on the planet than people and most have the ability to quickly snap an image or video at a moment's notice. This is usually just very cool and convenient. You got that great shot of your baby that you can share with Grandma. You captured your friend in the perfect pose for that one moment. However, this convenience comes at a cost.

In 2010, the Lower Merion school district in a suburb of Philadelphia, Pennsylvania, had a policy that encouraged students to take home school-owned laptops to do their homework. Many students took advantage of the program, finding it convenient to do schoolwork during breaks and at home overnight.[3] At odd times, however, the computers' green lights near the webcam would flicker on, seeming to indicate that their cameras had been enabled. Indeed, the school district had installed spyware on the laptops, allowing it to remotely access the webcams. Such spyware was normally used for recovering stolen laptops by attempting to identify the criminal and the location of the pilfered device, but the school district instead used these cyber tools

to monitor some of its students at home. Student Blake
Robbins, then 15, was photographed more than 400 times
in two weeks, sometimes as he slept.[4] Another student was
photographed more than 8,000 times over the course of
about six months.[5] These recordings were made public only
when Robbins was called into the assistant principal's office
and accused of taking drugs. A screenshot showed him holding what the school said were pills. Robbins contended that
he was actually eating Mike and Ike candies. Two lawsuits
were settled for $610,000, and at least one more is pending.

Although using a webcam to capture videos and images
of schoolchildren without parental consent is unsettling
and immoral, undisclosed video recording is not necessarily illegal. Many of today's eavesdropping laws cover only
wiretapping by surveillance tools that have an aural aspect.
As long as no audio is transmitted or recorded, these surveillance laws may not apply.[6]

And indeed, in some circumstances, our civil liberties
may actually be better protected through video recording
of public occurrences. Consider the case of Simon Glik. A
Boston-area criminal defense attorney, Glik had just finished
a clerkship in 2007 with the probate court and happened
to witness an arrest in Boston Common (a public park in
downtown Boston). Ten feet away from the suspected drug
offender, Glik observed punches thrown and a choke hold.
When he felt the police were using unnecessary force, he
pulled out his cell phone and photographed the arrest.
Afterward, an officer approached Glik and asked him if his
phone had "recording capabilities." When he confirmed
that it did, the officer seized his phone and arrested him. In

2011, the U.S. Court of Appeals for the First Circuit ruled that Glik had a right to video record the police in action. Part of the reasoning was that he was not "secretly recording" but rather "openly recording"—openly holding up his phone to capture the event.[7] Charges against him were later dropped, but Glik sued the officers and the City of Boston for violating his First Amendment rights. A settlement in 2012 netted Glik $170,000.

A similar event happened in Baltimore in 2010. Christopher Sharp observed Baltimore officers forcibly arresting his female friend at the Preakness Stakes horse race. The woman was shoved to the ground, and a pool of blood from her mouth was clearly visible. Sharp used his phone to video record the melee. Afterward, the officers ordered him to surrender his device. He did and the officers briefly left with his phone. They later returned and delivered his cell phone with all the recordings on his device deleted, including personal videos of his son at sporting events. Sharp later participated in a $250,000 settlement.[8]

Regarding this event, the U.S. Department of Justice officially weighed in during the 2012 litigation process on "whether private citizens have a First Amendment right to record police officers in the public discharge of their duties, and whether officers violate citizens' Fourth and Fourteenth Amendment rights when they seize and destroy such recordings without a warrant or due process." The Justice Department "urge[d] th[e] Court to answer both of those questions in the affirmative."[9]

The Baltimore Police Department (BPD) later released a policy spelling out citizens' right to "video record, photograph, and/or audio record BPD Members while BPD Members are conducting official business or while acting in an official capacity in any public place unless such recordings interfere with police activity."[10] This policy apparently goes both ways. In 2015, the BPD equipped more than 150 police officers with body cameras to record their interactions with the public to create a record of police interactions with civilians.[11]

The use of surveillance cameras is ubiquitous in not only the United States but many other nations. In London, perhaps the most "Big Brother" city in the world, there are approximately 51,000 police-run cameras[12] with more than 500,000 publicized privately operating cameras always watching.[13] Private citizens, company owners, and governments are continually installing additional cameras to monitor activities in areas of interest. Web-connected security systems have now gone mainstream, and can be installed by a home user for a modest investment. At least some of these systems are already capturing images of individuals in their residences, even if unintentionally. Furthermore, with the growing number of surveillance devices like smartphones in our pockets, conflicts over what can be recorded and what is public will continue.

What You Record Is Not Necessarily Just Yours: Data Storage and Aggregation

Even more significant is that these recorded images and sounds are no longer stored on individual devices but are usually uploaded to the cloud, essentially a mammoth server farm accessed through an end point device. Not only can these clouds cache huge amounts of digital data at a modest cost, but the aggregation of that data in a linked-data-storage environment also means that the cloud provider (or a government agency through legal process) can search the entire field of data and extract and aggregate all the information that pertains to a single individual. Modern analytic tools make such searches practical and inexpensive. That accumulated information can be effortlessly disseminated around the world and cached forever.

More and more of this aggregation happens automatically, as a convenience. Software writers think of convenient things, either for themselves or for the users of their software, and add them in because it's simple to do. As an example, the default setting for many digital images, whether taken on a mobile device such as an iPhone or a professional camera, includes a significant amount of information in addition to the actual image. This records not only time and date, but also things like aperture setting and flash information for the photographer to review. Many images also record where the image was taken, as reported by an onboard GPS system. This "extra" information is metadata—recorded for the photographers to pinpoint where they were when the image was recorded, or to enable them to re-create the camera settings in future photographs.

Metadata may sound harmless, but others can easily review it. Free software tools, such as Jeffrey Friedl's Exif viewer,[14] were capable of tracking the location of the image.[15] Celebrities who accidentally forget to turn off this feature can reveal the location of their private residences. This was the case with Adam Savage, star of the popular TV show *MythBusters*, when he tweeted out a picture of his car just prior to leaving for work with the comment "Now it's off to work." Unknowingly, he had just revealed to the world the location of his home.[16]

Location data is not always so obvious as GPS coordinates. Supermodel Hannah Davis posted a photo of herself in costume on Halloween in 2015. Although the photo contained no geolocation information, a distinctive curtain and carpet pattern in the image allowed paparazzi photographers to track the celebrity and await her exit from the building.[17]

We live in an age when there is a camera on every corner because everyone carries one. We have become the paparazzi. In our eagerness to take a picture of that celebrity we spotted on the corner and post it on Facebook or Instagram, we don't stop to think that we are providing a real-time tracker to others. In fact, software has been developed to help stalk celebrities. In 2010, a website and application named JustSpotted was launched. The tool allowed users to track celebrities' whereabouts from Twitter and other social media sightings.[18]

Twitter, however, wants celebrities who "tweet" to feel safe doing so. The company cut JustSpotted's access to the "firehose data feed of all public tweets."[19] Interestingly, a year later, the entire JustSpotted development team was hired by Google to work on the Google+ social platform.[20] It appears that social media data owners and larger technology companies have begun to self-regulate, creating new norms regarding the use of social media data on the internet. Today, however, because that data exists, simply shutting down one celebrity-stalker application does not prevent others from stalking.

The elimination of the transaction costs of these functions has eliminated information friction and its ameliorative effects. What happens in Vegas no longer stays in Vegas, but can be combined with stored records and reports of behavior anywhere and disseminated around the world, or be rediscovered years later. The costs of public acts have been greatly magnified.

Wittingly and Unwittingly, People Are Invading Their Own Privacy

Many people, without full understanding, place personal information in communications, email, data storage (i.e., the cloud), and social media services that allow the operator or owner of the service to examine, retain, and even market the data generated. Moreover, as online and communications activity increasingly moves from hardwire lines to wireless, it is easier for third parties to intercept and capture data when that data is transmitted wirelessly through the air than when one must physically insert hardware to eavesdrop. Thus, there is the increasing likelihood of "digital leakage" through which outsiders can intercept metadata, communications, and even physical location data on an almost continuous basis.

Most people are aware that personal data uploaded to social media is accessible to the service provider, at least in order to monitor and increase the efficiency of the service, but also to enable direct or third-party marketing of various unrelated goods and services. It might be considered a convenience that the boots you looked at on another website are now listed as on sale in a Facebook ad.

Less obvious may be those internet service providers that monitor not only web searches but also the content of email to develop raw data for targeted advertising. Even more obscure are the various retail and other commercial "loyalty" card programs and various credit card promotions that allow the card issuer to record not only what has been purchased with the loyalty or credit card, but also where and when.

Now imagine that your search data, email data, and purchase data were combined so that an analyst could correlate the frequency and extent of your searches with actual purchases. Or that one could predict from your correlated posts, social media, and email references who is most likely to influence you to make a purchase. No need to imagine—it's being done! Both Google and Facebook offer their paying business clients data that shows correlations between viewing online advertisements and purchases. The most informative data shows purchases completed sometimes days and weeks after an online ad has been viewed. This information is gathered from your clicks on ads and then visits to brick-and-mortar stores while you are logged in to Google or Facebook apps.[21] Did you use Google Maps to get you to the store? Were you checking Facebook posts while there? This information can be and is being used to provide you with targeted advertising.

Of course, there are more than commercial benefits from accessing and analyzing this kind of data. Political campaign consultants increasingly seek information about behavior that correlates with political preferences, both as a way of more efficiently purchasing political ads and to help shape candidate messaging. During the 2012 presidential race, the Obama campaign purchased cable and satellite viewer data and correlated it with profiles of persuadable voters (derived from social media postings and other data) to determine which programming was most often viewed by people sympathetic to President Obama. Using software dubbed the "Optimizer," campaign officials were able to target "persuadable" voters who tuned in to specific TV programs at specific times. Rather than estimate the effects of ads across a segment of the voting population (such as those of a certain gender and age), the Obama campaign was able to maximize advertising dollars by "microtargeting" individual voters.[22]

Campaigns are getting more sophisticated. In the 2016 primary season, for instance, one data intelligence firm that sells targeted advertising information to large companies compiled voter traits from smartphones and concluded that people who liked to grill or work on their lawns were highly likely to vote for Donald Trump in Iowa.[23] To create individualized voter profiles, campaigns are gathering more and more information from a vast array of sources—voting records, unions, advocacy groups, political parties, social media, and paid-for consumer data, to name just a few.

Campaigns want to build a profile of every person of voting age to predict and influence votes.[24] Data footprints are also valuable to service providers. Modern mobile phones, automobiles, radio frequency identification (RFID) cards, and fobs all generate information about the location of the person holding the object. There are many reasons to do this: it may be crucial to the service being provided, or might be useful in an emergency, so warnings or assistance can be rendered. But again, there are collateral uses. One is to identify when a device holder is shopping, so targeted advertisements or discount offers can be texted to the telephone or communicated in some other way. In the aggregate, this kind of information can be used to map someone's routine schedule and pattern of life.

By the same token, there is now a proliferation of fitness-tracking devices that monitor physical activity, heart rate, calories burned, distance traveled, and even blood sugar levels. As this data is uploaded to cloud storage, it becomes available and valuable for marketing. According to a 2014 Federal Trade Commission (FTC) study, 12 mobile health applications or devices transmit data to 76 third parties.[25] Some of that information passed along can be traced back to specific individuals. Indeed, these difficult-to-identify third parties may receive key health information, such as meal or diet information, gender, and medical-symptom search history. The FTC report understatedly summarizes this: "There are significant privacy implications where health routines, dietary habits, and symptom searches are capable of being aggregated using identifiers unique to that consumer."

Indeed, as technology has become more sophisticated, it has become possible for data companies to surreptitiously communicate with multiple separate devices to gain a picture of almost everything a consumer watches, reads, physically and electronically visits, or purchases. As the Center for Democracy and Technology wrote in administrative comments to the FTC, the ability of data merchants to attribute activities on multiple devices to a single person forms a detailed portrait of that person's activities.[26] Specifically, the Center for Democracy and Technology report mentions that "by tracking individuals across devices, marketers can create complete and detailed profiles of each individual user and recognize long-term shopping or behavioral patterns." FTC research further showed that 87 percent of 100 popular websites had cross-device trackers embedded.[27] This capability has been enhanced through tracking technology that pairs multiple devices within range. Once paired, the devices' camera, microphone, and other sensors can be employed to track a user's behavior. This technology is part of Google's popular Chromecast system and embedded in many smartphone applications without the user's knowledge.

With existing technology, it is possible to assemble from individuals' social media, email, mobile device, fitness-wearable technologies, and automobile vast amounts of information about their interests, physical fitness, daily routine, driving behavior, and consumer preferences, and perhaps even their politics. For better or worse, an outside party could determine what you eat, drink, watch, and read; how often you exercise; and where and how you drive. A third party could gather information on whether you purchase a coffee before you drive, whether you are eating more fat and skipping the gym, and whether you are an aggressive driver who takes a high-traffic route to work.

Increasingly, a wide variety of businesses are relying on just such data to assemble comprehensive portraits of customers and clients. A German financial services firm assesses the creditworthiness of online borrowers by examining social media behavior, language analytics, internet browsing history, and similar information furnished or agreed to by the prospective customer.[28] In one sense, this use of analytics allows a lender to look beyond the traditional criteria of repayment and credit history so individuals who might not meet normal credit standards can demonstrate their reliability. Of course, that assessment is only as good as the algorithm on which it relies.

Likewise, as previously described, insurers are beginning to adopt the same data-rich approach in underwriting and pricing risk. A number of insurers currently use "telematics" to monitor car driving. Mileage, hours on the road, time of day, speed, brake activation, and other statistics are gathered and uploaded in near real-time to company servers from onboard diagnostic information. Most of the data generated flows from a device that drivers agree to connect to their automobiles in order to qualify for a discount.

One insurer has more than 750,000 such devices already installed in the field, and the numbers are growing. The company has also recently secured patents for a much more comprehensive surveillance system that could track a driver's every move. Through cameras and sensors, it would be able to track not only car performance and operation (did you signal at that last intersection?), but also driver heart rate and blood pressure, and occupant information. The company may also be free to use the data and sell it to third-party companies that provide anything from credit ratings to personal health insurance.[29] Again, the potential benefit to the consumers in losing privacy is that they are rewarded for good driving behavior rather than being lumped into a risk category based upon actuarial generalizations derived from age and other general factors. The risk, however, is that algorithms will be flawed or people whose work or living circumstances require them to drive at certain times or in certain places will be systematically penalized.

Of course, in most of the foregoing instances, participation by the customer is voluntary. But what happens when failure to provide the data becomes cause for a penalty?[30] For example, your insurer may raise your premiums unless you consent to furnishing much of your personal data. Or imagine that an employer rejects your job application because it finds your absence of social media activity suspicious.

Perhaps the most remarkable example of potentially mandatory data collection as a means of social control is the effort currently under way in China. Commercial companies now rate creditworthiness based not only on financial behavior but also on information gathered about how people spend their time and what they purchase. The Chinese government is considering requiring an application of such techniques to establish a social credit score. This would incorporate not just economic activity but also what internet sites are visited and the social credit ranking of one's friends.[31] As such scores are increasingly displayed and relied upon by users, they will exert social pressure that could be a powerful incentive to modify behavior. Citizens will become their own social-behavior monitors.

It's Not Just About You;
It's About What Can Be Done to You

The internet revolution of recent years encompasses not just the huge quantity of information generated by individuals. Another element of this colossal change is how many systems in the physical world are operated through digitally driven controls hosted in internet networks. These systems both generate data, including things such as energy usage, and guide the performance of the system. Potentially, an interloper on the internet could affect, damage, or destroy systems controlling transportation, energy utilities, and medical procedures. Or such a trespasser could execute financial transactions.

Attacks like these are more than a theoretical possibility. In 2000, Vitek Boden, an individual denied employment by the Maroochy Shire Council in Queensland, Australia, turned his knowledge of radio-controlled SCADA systems into hacker tools. Boden remotely penetrated the control system for a sewage-treatment plant in Queensland. After taking over the plant control system, he caused the release of millions of liters of raw sewage into rivers and nearby picnic areas.[32]

In 2011, a public water utility company in Texas was hacked by someone using Russian internet addresses. The attack manipulated the control system and led to the burnout of a pump and theft of customer usernames and passwords.[33] The Department of Homeland Security (DHS), called in to investigate the incident, treated the issue as nothing but a pump failure with no risk to critical infrastructure. This DHS assessment so enraged another hacker, known as "pr0f," that he determined to prove an attack on the water treatment system was possible. He hacked the system, grabbed screenshots from the control-system software, and published the results online. Unlike the attacker who used Russian internet addresses, pr0f intentionally did not cause any physical damage to the plant. He also said that the hack wasn't really a hack, because the system was protected with a basic three-character password. "Connecting interfaces to your SCADA machinery to the internet" was stupid, pr0f said, adding that it "required almost no skill and could be produced by a two year old."[34]

Sometime in 2014, an unknown group of hackers penetrated the business information system of a German steel mill and made their way through the internal network, eventually getting into the control system for a furnace. They manipulated the system to make it impossible to properly shut the furnace, causing "massive damage" to the system,[35] and in 2015 and 2016, as earlier described, the electricity went out during the Christmas season for hundreds of thousands of Ukrainians whose electric grid was hacked and shut down, probably by Russian hackers carrying on the hybrid warfare campaign against the Ukrainian government.[36]

The risks need not be life-threatening. In 2012, the world's most valuable company, the Saudi Arabian Oil Company, known as Saudi Aramco, was hacked. An inserted virus spread through the company's network and indiscriminately wiped over 30,000 hard drives. Many employees were away for the Muslim holiday of Laylat al Qadr (Night of Power), ensuring that the virus would cause maximum destruction. The few on-site employees noticed their "computers were acting weird; screens started flickering; files began to disappear; some computers just shut down without explanation."[37] Without access to database information, business transactions halted. Gasoline trucks seeking to load up and distribute fuel at stations were turned away because pay services were offline. Production services remained constant at 9.5 million barrels a day because of automation. To restore its corporate network systems, Saudi Aramco placed representatives directly on factory floors of hard-drive manufacturers in Southeast Asia. A premium price was paid to secure the first 50,000 hard drives off the manufacturing line and to bring the corporate network back online. Despite immense resources and access to IT experts, it took Saudi Aramco almost two weeks to restore services and five months to rebuild a more secure corporate system.[38]

The Internet of Things: You Ain't Seen Nothing Yet

The destructive risk is not limited to large digitally driven infrastructure connected to the network. At conferences over the past several years, researchers have demonstrated the ability to use wireless connections to interfere with or halt operation of automobiles or medical devices, such as pacemakers and insulin pumps. The prospect of wirelessly connected networks of millions of mechanical devices, including thermostats, cameras, refrigerators, and automobiles, is often called, as mentioned earlier, the "internet of things."

In 2015, two security researchers hacked into a 2014 Jeep Cherokee and were able to take control of the vehicle's steering wheel, briefly disable the brakes, and turn off its engine. Through a wireless entertainment and navigation system, they achieved internet access to thousands of other Jeeps, allowing them to control these vehicles from almost anywhere. Other researchers have identified multiple entry points into automobiles, including computers that interface with dashboard displays and air bags, which in turn allow access to transmissions, engines, and steering. Automobiles with voice-activated entertainment or Bluetooth can be penetrated so that the microphone records and transmits clandestinely by remote activation.[39]

The threat of remotely controlling or disabling vehicles is not merely a research activity. In 2010, an employee fired by the Texas Auto Center in Austin used cyber hacking to retaliate against his erstwhile employer and its customers. The company had embedded its cars with a device that would disable the ignition and trigger loud honking of the horn as a way of penalizing customers who were behind in their payments—a kind of high-tech repossession. The ex-employee hacked into more than 100 automobiles, shut down their ignitions, and triggered their horns.[40]

Another potential hazard is posed by medical devices and implants that are wirelessly connected to networks, allowing medical monitoring and updating after insertion into the human body. In 2015, students at the University of Alabama infiltrated the wireless pacemaker in a demonstration dummy and administered potentially lethal shocks remotely. It was precisely this fear that led former vice

president Dick Cheney's cardiologist to disable the wireless feature on Cheney's pacemaker. Other researchers have
demonstrated that wirelessly enabled drug-infusion implants
can be remotely manipulated to affect dosage.[41]

These research experiments demonstrate that the vulnerability of personal information (the issue of *data confidentiality*) and the vulnerability of control systems (the issue of
data integrity) are exacerbated by the data-connected internet
of things. This phenomenon opens a larger surface area
for interfering with physical systems as well as generates
enormous data about personal behavior. Even though you
are totally unaware, your car and fridge could be gathering
information about your daily routine and interests.

As microprocessors on chips have dramatically increased
their processing power, more computing capability is being
embedded in even small appliances. These can be networked
together to create smart devices, as part of the internet of
things. Increasingly, utilities are deploying the smart grid,
wirelessly connecting thermostats to the utility to measure
usage patterns and allow energy supplies to be adjusted,
with precision based on need. Companies are working on
clocks, kitchen appliances, and other household products
that monitor consumer behavior to turn on your coffee
machine moments before you wake up; warn you when you
are low on supplies; order groceries for the week; and allow
you to remotely operate your locks and lights so that you
need not be home to admit a visitor or to check that your
residence is secure.

Amazon has successfully marketed and released
a product called Echo. This device is an interactive,

internet-connected, voice-enabled speaker. Simply ask, and it will search the internet for an answer, tell you the weather, play music, or schedule your day. Amazon is also marketing a product called the Dash Button that can be placed near where you use a product in the house.[42] When you run out of the product (for example, laundry detergent), you push the Dash Button and it automatically generates an order, rapidly shipping the replacement to your door. No more writing down a list and going to the store!

An internet-connected oven called June uses overhead high-definition cameras to recognize the type of food you are attempting to cook.[43] It suggests cooking times and has built-in sensors to improve cooking performance. You can even watch the HD camera from your smartphone if you want to see what your cookies look like from the other room. Phillips Corporation makes internet-connected lighting systems that you can control from your smartphone. The system recognizes when you return home and will turn the lights on for you. In addition, you can control the lighting from anywhere in the world.

August Home, acquired by the global lockmaker Assa Abloy in 2017, makes a series of house locks that connect to existing hardware but allow for hands-free unlocking and locking through a cell phone–enabled connection.[44] The door will unlock as you approach and lock behind you. It will also track those who have entered and left using the digital lock. Hilton Hotels is syncing its door-locking system with a phone application to allow guests to check in and open their room door without needing to stop at the front desk for a key.[45]

Among the dangers of these networked devices are unwanted visitors hacking into your home and determining when you are away and what your daily patterns are. Several years ago, the U.S. Chamber of Commerce was penetrated by what appear to have been Chinese hackers entering through a vulnerability in an internet-connected, energy-saving smart thermostat.[46] The attackers had access to everything in the Chamber of Commerce network for months, including trade policy secrets.[47] It was not until the FBI identified the intrusion and notified the Chamber of Commerce that the hack was shut down.[48] More recently, the manufacturers of a remote system for operating lamps and other plug-in devices were warned that flaws in the code on these devices would allow outsiders to gain not only control of the device attached to the remote switch, but also access to any other device connected to the same wireless network. This could enable hackers to remotely control home appliances, and burglars to know when people are home.[49] To take another example, parents in Ohio using an internet-connected baby monitor were awoken by the sound of a man shouting, "Wake up, baby!" The monitor had been easily hacked because the default password had not been changed.

Researchers have also demonstrated that a networked refrigerator can be hacked and used to send out floods of nuisance advertising—spam.[50] Hotel locks and home alarms have also been hacked.[51]

Even children's toys are not immune. In this book's introduction, I portrayed a child's doll as a means of collecting large amounts of data on a family. That scenario is not improbable. Mattel's Hello Barbie doll was wirelessly enabled so that a child's statements could be relayed to a server to prompt a realistic response, as if it were a real conversation. Initially, the connection was left unprotected, meaning that it could be spoofed—that is, a hacker could turn it into a listening device or, worse yet, directly initiate a conversation with the child.[52]

Despite the increase of these computer-enabled, -connected devices, they remain among the most vulnerable hacker targets in the cyber ecosystem. Each of these internet-connected devices is enabled by a miniature embedded, very capable computer processor and an operating system that is targeted to perform a small number of functions. As a consequence, the processor is not likely to be protected by antivirus or other methods, and may not be capable of being updated. Processors are often not configured or supported to allow for corrections in flawed software code or vulnerabilities. In fact, computer printers are a popular target of hackers seeking entry into a network.[53] The printers' processors, memory, and network connections are rarely updated, making them easy prey. When was the last time you updated the embedded software (called firmware) on your printer? If vulnerable smart devices are not separated from critical nodes on the network, a malicious infection can rapidly spread throughout the network, avoiding any network perimeter defenses.

Chapter Four

RECONFIGURING PRIVACY AND SECURITY IN THE DATA 3.0 UNIVERSE

The policy and legal implications of the Data 3.0 revolution affect at least three sets of actors: individual citizens and enterprises who link to the internet as users; governments that approach the internet from a security standpoint; and private technology and data companies that operate or provide services on the internet.

Individuals and most commercial enterprises generate increasing volumes of data about themselves—both deliberately and as an incident to their daily activities—but few understand the full scope of what is online. Thus, third parties who access the data have the potential to monitor and obtain enormous quantities of private information about individuals and enterprises: their communications, their plans, their behavior, and even their viewing and reading habits. Further, there are increased opportunities to victimize users of the internet through crime, intellectual property theft, and even terrorism. These changes pose a significant challenge to our privacy, as well as to safety and security.

Governments also face these new vulnerabilities through the internet, while at the same time gaining vastly increased opportunities for surveillance and espionage. An image on the National Security Agency website showing the new Utah Data Center announces: "Welcome to the Utah Data Center" followed by the words, "If you have nothing to hide, you have nothing to fear."[1] We all have some things we may want to hide, at least temporarily, and these aren't necessarily illegal or illicit activities. We may not wish to anger our neighbors with our personal beliefs, enthusiasm, or passions.

We get along better as humans when we communicate from a position of common understanding. We all know that conversations appropriate at the dinner table or in the bedroom are not always appropriate with a public audience. It is not a bad thing to allow for places of private individual expression where ideas can be explored and challenged and beliefs solidified or disseminated.

Government as Both a Protector and an Exploiter of Your Data

By law, the government collects and houses large volumes of personal information. As government programs expand to include social service payments, health programs, educational loans, and the like, the ability to maintain the privacy and security of citizenship data becomes more critical; the loss of that data can expose citizens to risk of fraud, blackmail, or coercion. A dramatic example is the recent penetration of the U.S. Office of Personnel Management. This breach is calculated to have harvested over 25 million sets of federal government employment applications, including almost 20 million detailed background investigations and over 1 million sets of fingerprints. Not only does this violation expose individuals to risk of fraud and blackmail, but it also may effectively block employees from engaging in undercover intelligence-collection missions for the U.S. government.

Indeed, the Office of Personnel Management data theft shows how modern data technology has transformed the ability of nation-states to gather huge amounts of information through spying. Absconding with millions of personnel files would never have been feasible or even worthwhile as recently as a decade or so ago. First, collecting, duplicating, and transporting that data would have been impossible. (Imagine a Cold War Soviet agent spending hours at the Xerox machine or with a mini-camera copying files.) Now, by contrast, after only a few minutes, terabytes of data can be downloaded onto a thumb drive and carried away in a pants pocket.

Even more important, this data would have been of no interest in the 20th century because no team of analysts could ever have correlated it to identify patterns or threads that would enable detection of undercover or non–official cover agents. The advent of extensive data analytics has allowed this kind of trove of information to be worth stealing in the first place. In that sense, the data analytics revolution has made routine information worth obtaining through espionage.

Beyond the risk of exposure of confidential information is the risk of data integrity. As government operational functions—such as insurance enrollment and even voting—move online, the risk that a compromise of data integrity will affect the core operation of government also increases. Indeed, the Chinese have explicitly adopted as part of their military doctrine the concept of information warfare. This concept involves targeting an enemy's military and societal information structures to interfere with the enemy's war-fighting capability.

In 1988, Dr. Shen Weiguang, known as the father of Chinese information warfare theory, gave a lecture in which he described the future battlefield as invisible. It would be one where "virus-infected microchips" affected weapon systems. Logic bombs on self-destructing microchips could be seeded for future use against enemies by preparing their weapons to be ineffective.[2] This recalls Sun Tzu's ancient *Art of War* concept of destroying "the enemy's will to launch a war or wage a war."[3]

Information warfare is not theoretical. In 2008, the Russians attacked Georgia's government communications network to support ground operations during the military invasion of Georgian South Ossetia.

The government, therefore, has an increasing need to secure its data and its control systems on the internet, even as the vectors for attack have expanded with the surface area of the internet and the proliferation of entry points. That is why every presidential administration since the 1990s has emphasized the cybersecurity mission. In 2016, the director of national intelligence identified cyberattacks as *the* top national security threat.

Even more recently, Russian operatives have used hacking in an effort to subvert the electoral process in the United States and Europe. As the U.S. intelligence community has publicly confirmed, in the 2016 presidential election, Russian hacking groups penetrated and stole emails from the Hillary Clinton campaign; these were later made public to embarrassing effect. Other investigations into voter databases in 39 states revealed penetration or probing and potential compromise of voter data systems.[4] And these "information operations"—subversion through selective or distorted release of information—are not limited to the United States. In recent years, criminal hackers possibly linked to Russian groups have accessed the databases of German political-party think tanks and even the German Bundestag. The very mechanisms of democratic government have become cyber targets.

But the same technology that increases risk to government also enhances the government's defensive capabilities. As data and communications move from telephone and radio to include online transmissions, the opportunities to intercept or harvest data increase exponentially. This sort of collection is critical to defending against the sort of cyberattack described above, as well as against physical attacks by international terrorists or "lone wolves." So, on the one hand, the increased risks posed by the internet underscore the importance of governments taking steps to protect their citizens, including monitoring threats and attacks online. At the same time, there is more opportunity for governments to abuse these capabilities for repressive purposes.

As explained in the previous chapter, private enterprises that furnish internet services or that collect and hold data present an even newer challenge to traditional social expectations about privacy. Many of the new companies with the highest market capitalization in the world, such as Google and Facebook, base their businesses partly on the ability to harvest, analyze, and market data generated over the internet. Sometimes the data is generated by active and knowing user choice; at other times it is a by-product of consumer or enterprise activity and is unbeknownst to the user. In many ways, private data companies now exceed government in their capacity to collect, integrate, analyze, and use data about individuals. It has become increasingly difficult for people to preserve their privacy without disconnecting from what has become an almost indispensable utility of modern life.

The challenge becomes how to adapt 20th-century Data 2.0 legal and policy structure to the new circumstances of Data 3.0.

Protecting Your Data Depends on Who Holds It: The Third-Party Doctrine

Under Data 2.0, the relatively clear distinction between private and public communications meant that legal restrictions were rather high for government surveillance directly targeting an individual's communications. However, when that data was in the possession of someone other than the targeted individual, it got minimal legal protection. Thus, under the so-called Third-Party Doctrine, information voluntarily accessed by or conveyed to a third party, like telephone billing records in the possession of a telephone company (an example of metadata), got limited protection.

Smith v. Maryland illustrates this point. In the late 1970s in Baltimore, Patricia McDonough was robbed. She saw the man who robbed her as well as a 1975 Monte Carlo at the scene of the crime. She gave these details to the police. After the robbery, McDonough started receiving threatening calls from a man who identified himself as the robber. During one phone call, the man asked her to go out onto her front porch. When she did, she saw a 1975 Monte Carlo driving by. She gave the license plate number to the police, who were able to figure out that the car belonged to Michael Lee Smith.[5]

The next day, the police got the telephone company to install a pen register—a mechanical device that tracks electrical impulses—to record the numbers dialed from Smith's phone. Through the pen register, the police discovered that Smith had in fact placed the threatening calls to McDonough. The police followed up with a search of Smith's home, which revealed a phone book highlighting Patricia McDonough's name. Smith was eventually convicted for the robbery and sentenced to six years in prison.

On appeal, Smith argued that any evidence from the pen register should be excluded because the government failed to get a warrant, as is required to intercept conversations (under *Katz*). The Supreme Court held that the pen register did not invade any property interest since it was installed at the telephone company, not at Smith's home, and that Smith did not have a "legitimate expectation of privacy" in numbers dialed on his phone. The court noted that telephone users "realize" they voluntarily give the dialed numbers to the telephone company to place their calls. Further, phone books typically contain a notice that the phone company can help the police in identifying threatening phone calls.[6]

Smith asserts that individuals do not have a reasonable expectation of privacy in information that they voluntarily convey to third parties. Based on *Smith* and other court cases, an individual could be followed and photographed in public streets without limit, and the government could make use of that information for any legitimate purpose. Under the same principle, records generated by or transferred to a bank or phone company receive less protection than that afforded to the same documents when they are in the hands of the original creator or owner.

But in these days of Data 3.0, data collected in public spaces or by third parties is exponentially greater in volume, comprehensiveness, and persistence because of the lack of information friction. Also, with modern big data analytics, that data is susceptible to far more revealing insight into a person's thoughts and behavior. For example, while historically an individual might have been photographed periodically in a public square or even followed over a period of time by law enforcement, under modern technology, one can aggregate video, cell phone data, locational GPS data, and other information to create a virtual 24/7 map of that person's activities and associations.

Likewise, third-party data—such as individual phone and bank records, if collected at sufficient scale and combined with similar data generated by others—can be analyzed under algorithms that generate a full picture of an individual's actions and beliefs, and even likely future behavior. A remarkable example of these government capabilities is a software program operated by the Fresno Police Department's Real Time Crime Center. It assigns suspects a threat score that rates their dangerousness, much as a credit score rates creditworthiness. The system scours millions of public data entries, such as property records, commercially available databases, criminal records, social media postings and other data, video and license plate readings, and cell site location information (CSLI) downloaded from cell towers. Based on this and other data—all observable in public—the software tool assigns a risk warning (green, yellow, or red) to those persons who score above a certain level.[7]

Or take the example of Elk Grove, California, a Sacramento suburb that installed more than 100 camera feeds across the city. The video is sent directly to police department servers, allowing officer review at any moment. Historically, such a large number of surveillance devices would be only as good as the number of police officers watching them. This has changed with data analytics software. Modern video analytic tools allow officers to use "facial recognition, license plate readers, and object-based searches."[8] Officers can perform searches across weeks of video streams within seconds, looking for specific license plate numbers or for the face of a suspected criminal. Numerous officers are no longer required to monitor all the cameras. Just a few can monitor the entire city and be alerted, based upon chosen algorithms or areas with high crime rates.

Analytic capabilities also have remarkable counterterrorism potential. At a time when terrorists and criminals are increasingly sophisticated about encrypting or otherwise masking their communications, the collection of subtle metadata and other digital artifacts can be combined with use of geoanalytic software to predict where terrorists are likely to hide, build bombs, or train. For example, evasive steps to disguise calls from apparently random locations can be identified as the users' unconscious patterns emerge. These patterns are like behavioral tics that help triangulate where a terrorist lives and operates.

Finally, in order to function, cell phones must communicate with cell towers. As the phone carrier moves, the device continues to "register" with towers within the vicinity. Tools have been created that allow law enforcement officers to exploit this communication to target and locate criminals virtually anywhere. One of these devices, called a StingRay, mimics the action performed by a cell tower and sends/receives carrier signals by communicating with all cell phones in the vicinity. By comparing the unique identifying code number of each phone against others, officers can find cell phone locations with a high degree of accuracy.[9] These cell-site simulators are currently in the hands of law enforcement. History shows, however, that technologies tend to bleed outward and become available to all, making everyone vulnerable to being targeted for tracking and surveillance.

The Supreme Court Begins to Revise the Balance Between Government Access and Protecting Individuals' Data: *Jones* and *Riley*

From the standpoint of a citizen's physical and even online security, these new bulk-data tools make it easier for law enforcement to prevent crime and terrorism and, if necessary, to apprehend criminals and terrorists. But they also demonstrate that the amount of "public" data available to authorities about innocent civilians is vast when compared with what is traditionally regarded as protected by rights to privacy. What remains protected is almost negligible compared with what can be openly obtained and used by governments.

A calibration is overdue, and it is high time to consider what additional individual protections should be afforded to surveillance of even public behavior. In the face of the modern state, our challenge is to preserve enough individual control of personal information to secure personal autonomy.

Those issues have begun to be explored but have not been settled by the U. S. Supreme Court. In *United States v. Jones*, several justices raised the prospect that public surveillance on a large scale might warrant legal restrictions not currently applied. The facts of the case were straightforward, and initially it appeared to be a routine application of the principle that openly visible, public behavior gets minimal privacy protection.

In 2004, the FBI and Washington, D.C., police began to suspect that Antoine Jones, the owner of a nightclub, was trafficking narcotics. Although they had no valid search warrant, as part of their investigation the authorities attached a GPS device to a Jeep Cherokee owned by Jones's wife while it was parked at a public lot. Over 28 consecutive days, the device generated data about every movement of the Jeep, accurate to within 50 to 100 feet. The device yielded 2,000 pages of data.[10] The tracking showed the defendant's travel to a drug-stash house, where the authorities found 97 kilograms of cocaine, 1 kilogram of cocaine base, and over $800,000 in cash.[11] The defendant sought to suppress the evidence obtained from the GPS, declaring it a warrantless search, and his case worked its way up to the Supreme Court.

All nine justices agreed that tracking the automobile in public through the attached GPS was a search and that the evidence had to be barred because there was no warrant. But the various opinions demonstrated the fault line in analysis between the age of Data 2.0 and that of Data 3.0.

The majority of justices joined a narrowly drafted opinion that analyzed the search based on the physical placement of the GPS on the car. A minimal physical attachment was sufficient under traditional doctrine to constitute a trespass, which—as described above—was the rationale for privacy protection.

But several justices couched their objections not as a result of the physical trespass, but as a function of the long, unbroken duration of the surveillance. In their view, at the point where technology allowed public-place surveillance to exceed "reasonable expectations of privacy," an invasion of privacy under the Fourth Amendment had occurred.

For the first time, a number of justices said that activity that would be public if observed for a short duration could take on a privacy right if technology enabled the observation for an extended period. In essence, they found that technological elimination of practical constraints on constant physical surveillance changed how we should apply privacy protection. Put another way, the elimination of what I have termed information friction means that constant surveillance of a person in public spaces could actually amount to an invasion of privacy.

One justice went even beyond this and suggested that perhaps there should be a further threshold before certain machine algorithms would be allowed to analyze such data. As Justice Sonia Sotomayor explained, because of modern analytic capabilities, perhaps the use of information that is disclosed to third parties now deserves additional privacy limitations under the Constitution.[12] Essentially, these justices raised the question of whether Data 3.0 has so fundamentally transformed what is public that new protections for personal freedom are needed.

Subsequent decisions by the courts have been divided over whether location tracking based upon the collection of large amounts of cell phone location data is worthy of new legal restraints. Such information gathering might require a warrant either because its duration is excessive or because the cell phone is carried into private spaces (like homes or offices).[13] In May 2016, the U.S. Court of Appeals for the Fourth Circuit decided that a warrant was not needed to allow the government to track the location of smartphone users.[14] The court reasoned that, under the traditional Third-Party Doctrine, smartphone users had already consented to the service. Since they had voluntarily given up their geolocation, the third-party service provider could then share that information with the government.[15] But to place this ruling in full context, note this: nearly two-thirds of American adults now own smartphones.[16] The Supreme Court has now heard arguments in *Carpenter v. United States*, a case involving whether judicial warrants are required to obtain cell phone locational data.[17] The decision in this case will determine the future of virtually continuous geolocation by U.S. authorities, although it has no effect on foreign governments. If the Court does not impose some warrant requirement on obtaining this data, the risk is that the use of this modern smartphone technology—originally a convenience, and quickly becoming for many a necessity—will begin to include an automatic government-tracking capability.

This data storage revolution was also at the core of the Supreme Court decision in *Riley v. California*.[18] The police arrested David Leon Riley after a traffic stop revealed loaded firearms in his car. The police seized Riley's cell phone and searched his contacts, messages, videos, and photographs. Based in part on this data, the government charged Riley with an unrelated previous shooting. Riley was convicted, and the California Court of Appeal affirmed, relying on the long-standing legal principle that items on the person or within reach of an arrested individual may be searched automatically by police, without a warrant or probable cause (the "search incident to arrest" doctrine). Other courts, including the First Circuit in a case called *United States v.*

Wurie, reached a different conclusion.[19] The Supreme Court granted an appeal to resolve the disagreement.[20] In *Riley*, the Supreme Court held in a unanimous opinion by Chief Justice Roberts that the police search of a cell phone during an arrest, absent exigent or emergency circumstances, needs a probable-cause warrant.[21] The Court reasoned that a cell phone search does not advance the two major government interests: officer safety and evidence preservation.[22] Police may not search a cell phone on the individual automatically at the time of arrest. The Court characterized cell phones as "minicomputers," emphasizing their significant difference from other objects on an arrestee's person.[23] The Court recognized that traditionally, items on the person of someone lawfully arrested can be searched without a judicial warrant because of the limited scope of the search (targeting only items carried by the person). But, as the Court observed, the data-storage capacity of mobile phones and the fact that these devices are often keys into vast quantities of data, stored in the cloud, change the nature of what is being searched. The *Riley* opinion did not decide whether there should be further judicial permission required before raw data properly seized by the police can also be subjected to an analytic algorithm.[24]

The *Riley* decision is an important one, but it does not resolve all privacy issues related to law enforcement's use of cell phone data. Lawmakers in New York have considered introducing a Textalyzer to enforce no-texting-while-driving laws, much the same way a Breathalyzer helps police stop drunk driving.[25] The device would allow police officers arriving on the scene of a traffic accident to determine whether a driver had been texting, emailing, or using other functions of a cell phone that New York State law prohibits because it requires two hands on the wheel. Although it would not allow a blanket search, the Textalyzer, if introduced, would almost certainly face a legal challenge, and *Riley* would come into play.

The storage issue arises in another area in which the government generally has broad authority to seize physical items: searches at the border. It has long been the case that at a port of entry, agents may search anything being carried into the country. The question becomes whether that also applies to cell phones and laptops, which, as the *Riley* opinion pointed out, have more storage capacity for information than an entire house.[26] As the Court explained in *Riley*, a cell phone search invades privacy interests substantially.[27] Cell phones may contain internet browsing history, historic location information, dating apps, or political affiliation information; that means they are sources of especially sensitive information.[28] Moreover, increasingly, much of this information is stored on the cloud—essentially a remotely located computer server or set of servers—rather than on the device itself. That means that the search of a cell phone can yield vast amounts of detailed personal information not even located on the phone. If information accessed through a device is actually kept on a server elsewhere in the United States through storage in the cloud, seizing and opening the device is akin to grabbing a traveler's house key and claiming authority to access his entire house.

The agency U.S. Customs and Border Protection (CBP) came under increasing scrutiny for its searches of personal cell phones at the border in early 2017,[29] prompting it to publicly reassert its authority to conduct searches of cell phones at the border and release statistics demonstrating the relatively small number of travelers affected by such searches.[30] The controversy prompted several senators to introduce a bill that would bar CBP from conducting cell phone searches for U.S. citizens and green card holders at the border and press the agency for clarification as to its policies on cell phone searches.[31] CBP later responded to Senate inquiries by clarifying that its search authority does not allow its agents to examine any data stored in the cloud, including social media.[32]

Not surprisingly, the courts have divided on the level of protection to be afforded in a border search of a cell phone or laptop. For example, a California federal court allowed a warrantless search of a cell phone for numbers and text messages, while a D.C. federal court suppressed a warrantless search of a laptop inspected at the border.[33] Eventually, even at the border—where courts have traditionally favored the government's interest in security over the individual's interest in privacy—the law must adapt, given the amount of data stored on laptops, computers, and other devices. Someday soon, even a border search of mobile devices should require a greater showing of probable cause and perhaps a judicial search warrant because the device is effectively the portal to a search of an individual's personal data held in databases all over the world.

The Data 3.0 Threat Environment

Before assuming that the universal response to Data 3.0 is in all instances to impose more restraint on government, consider that the new technologies we have described also magnify threats to individual citizens. Too much restraint on government use of new technology might tip the balance in favor of terrorists and criminals. Data 3.0 dramatically increases the ability of dangerous people to expand their network and gives them new vectors through which they can attack, injure, or even kill innocent civilians. Recent events have demonstrated that the internet is a recruiting and training tool for terrorists.

As detailed in a recent report by West Point's Combating Terrorism Center, ISIS recruits Americans and Europeans by identifying people who search or log on to certain websites. Reaching out to them to make friendly contact, ISIS then slowly grooms them as potential recruits. This process uses social media to encourage targeted recruits to isolate themselves from non-supporters and mainstream Muslims. Next come private messages to encourage migration to the Islamic State, lone-wolf attacks, or financial support.[34] According to a story in the *New York Times*, a 23-year-old woman named Alex who lived with her grandparents in Washington State started chatting online for hours every day with an ISIS fighter in Syria and other supporters.[35] They taught her the basics of Islam over Skype and sent her a gift certificate for $200 to an online Islamic bookstore, hijabs, chocolate, and eventually pamphlets with extreme interpretations of Islam. When Alex learned about a mosque five miles away from her home, she was discouraged from visiting it. Alex discussed religious justifications for suicide bombing with her interlocutors, and an ISIS supporter offered her a trip to Austria for an arranged marriage. Suspecting her recruitment, Alex's family intervened and called the FBI.[36]

Without the ability to follow and connect the dots linking a widely dispersed network, there is no reliable way to detect terrorists or recruits who, by definition, do not wear uniforms or identify themselves. As of early 2016, some 6,600 Westerners, men and women, including approximately 250 Americans, had traveled to Iraq or Syria to fight with or otherwise support ISIS. The average age of such recruits was 24.[37] In 2015, at least 60 people were arrested in the United States for criminal support of the Islamic State.[38]

Apart from recruiting and inspiring terrorists, the internet can be the actual means to carry out attacks that disrupt, corrupt, or even destroy data systems and the physical control systems connected to them. With the proliferation of the internet of things, the opportunities for destructive attacks have increased.

Recall the power grid hack in Ukraine. The power grid was disabled when the attacker hacked into the SCADA network, shutting off the control switches at approximately 30 substations and then wiping the control computers to make them useless. The attack caused control systems to go "suddenly blind," and to issue a fake report that made it seem that power was flowing while it actually had been shut off. A secondary phone disruption hack prevented technicians from getting updates by telephone. This prevented customers from calling in and reporting the power outage, further delaying the response to correct the system.[39]

In 2014 a version of the same malware used in the Ukraine attack, a BlackEnergy backdoor Trojan virus, was discovered to have been within the United States electric grid network since 2011.[40] Although the virus was removed when discovered, hackers continue to insinuate new variants of it into portions of the grid. And there is still debate over whether one virus is simply a means of reconnaissance or a latent destructive tool that can be activated remotely. The Ukrainians were in many ways lucky. The Ukrainian power grid is not as automated as the U.S. system is. Although physically remote, the manual switches existed in Ukraine for restoring the grid's operability. If its automated control system is damaged, the U.S. network may not be as easily restored.

The only way to detect and block the foregoing threats is to match the comprehensive "battle space" of the attackers on the network. There are two dimensions to this approach.

First, the government must have sufficient awareness of recruiting and other communications over the internet to be able to identify incipient threats. This means either the capability to collect public information or the legal authority, with appropriate safeguards, to intercept more private communications.

Second, to address instances where the internet itself is the vector of threat (espionage; reconnaissance; disruption or destruction of systems), the government needs the cyber equivalent of radar.

At the very least, the government must be able to monitor and evaluate packets of malware for critical infrastructure networks. Undue curtailment of that capability would cede the battle space to the enemy.

Additionally, tools that allow anonymization or that facilitate the deep web, like the Tor browser, potentially create a law-free zone in which illegal or terrorist activity can flourish. What should be the government's authority to penetrate the deep web and to identify those who wish to remain anonymous? As a corollary, how should the government deal with encryption, which can be used to mask threatening activity? Is it right that the government should use its tools to break encryption or to exploit vulnerabilities for intelligence collection purposes? To go further, should the law require service providers to keep a duplicate key for decryption purposes when presented with a lawful government or court order to do so? These questions are explained below.

Toward a Solution: Stages of Surveillance

One way to reconcile increased privacy concerns with today's government security imperatives is to unpack the stages of surveillance and to view the process as a continuum.

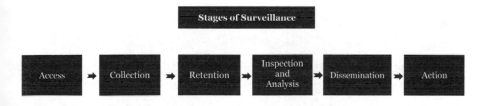

Access is the capability—unexercised—to collect data. It may include prepositioned infrastructure, preexisting legal arrangements, and the ability and expertise to decrypt any encrypted communications obtained. Access does not immediately compromise the privacy of data although, if misused, it could.

Collection is the process of obtaining data without inspecting or reviewing it. More and more, the government collects a great amount of information as a hedge—in case future review is needed. Advances in cheap storage capacity have made this possible.

Retention is the decision by an agency about how long to keep information that has been either collected or inspected. The longer an agency retains data, the greater capability it has to mine the data for patterns. But longer retention also means data is more vulnerable.

Inspection and Analysis is the point at which someone or something looks at and processes what is collected. In the intelligence world, often the pivotal moment of authorization is deemed to be not at collection but rather at the inspection stage. (Note the potential distinction between human and machine review; the machine might review data as a matter of course.) By shifting the pivotal moment from collection to inspection, the intelligence community is able to vacuum up information without triggering privacy protections until it reviews or acts on the data.

Dissemination is the decision to share the data from one entity (e.g., a collector) with another entity (e.g., a reviewer). Sharing data makes it available for more uses, and we may want to restrict some entities from using certain data. For instance, if the NSA collects communications data that includes U.S. person information, when can it share this data with domestic-facing agencies like the FBI? This question lies at the heart of the accusation by President

Donald Trump that intelligence agencies were improperly "unmasking," or revealing, the identities of his assistants who had been incidentally intercepted in communications with Russian officials.

Sharing data with more entities may also make that data more vulnerable.

Action occurs when an agency takes a step based on data collected, such as processing a claim, indicting a suspect, or targeting a terrorist. Restrictions on the use of the information or rules about what consequences may flow come into play. This includes the application of *predictive analytic techniques* to the raw data. When can an agency take datasets, use them to predict behavior about individual people, and then act on those predictions?

Looking at this continuum allows us to identify the points at which we can regulate the protection of individual autonomy. At each stage, we can agree to allow (or forbid) legal authorities to access, collect, retain, inspect, disseminate, or act on data.

The traditional U.S. surveillance policy to protect privacy has been to view the critical threshold as collection. Thus, constitutional case law largely turned on whether a warrant and probable cause were required to collect physical items or to intercept audio communications or record visual data. Once collection was permissible, however, there was little restriction on the retention, analysis, or further transmission of that data, although a federal statute, the Privacy Act of 1974, did limit the use and transmission of lawfully collected information to legitimate government purposes. In Europe, by contrast, not only collection but also retention and use are subject to separate legal restrictions (more on this below).

A legal model that treats the stages of the surveillance continuum with separate, more finely tuned restrictions will enable society to better accommodate both concerns about individual freedom and the simultaneous need for more advanced tools that protect security for all of us. This book urges that we facilitate potential access and even collection, while adding tougher restrictions upon the use, retention, and dissemination of data.

Access

Historically in the United States, when it came to wiretapping or video surveillance, there was little restriction on access (i.e., the government's ability to develop collection technology or to install it) provided there was no physical encroachment on private property. One exception to this principle arose in the mid-1990s, when there was a debate about whether telecommunications carriers should be required to ensure that new encryption technologies be modified to enable access for wiretapping if ordered by a court. In 1993, the Clinton White House introduced the "Clipper Chip," a microchip developed by the government that could be installed in telephones, providing encryption for private parties but still allowing government access. Before initiating an encrypted voice call, a Clipper Chip would send a digital signature to a "key escrow" so that the government could acquire the keys and decrypt the call.[41] The Clipper Chip generated a heated debate that anticipates today's encryption controversies: the government warned about lack of access, while privacy advocates, technology experts, and industry leaders opposed the measure as undermining trust in the privacy protections of U.S. products and services, and creating a backdoor for would-be hackers and criminals to exploit. A report by influential leaders in cryptography decried the Clipper Chip.[42] Ultimately, because of the controversy, no such requirement for the Clipper Chip was imposed. But in 2016, the FBI launched a similar effort to mandate that internet service providers and device manufacturers include a backdoor or duplicate key, so the government can decode encrypted data transmitted over the internet or held on devices like smartphones. The controversy over this effort has not yet been resolved.

The current, outdated legal framework is both underinclusive and overinclusive. For example, with the proliferation of data and modern analytics, information of no immediate obvious significance may gain significance in the context of subsequently acquired data from a wider set of sources. This may be crucial in tracing back links among terrorists or cyber criminals. If the original information was not collected as well as stored for later use, its value may be lost forever.

Another, but opposite, danger is that given the currently low threshold for collecting data about public behavior—through, say, video cameras widespread in many large cities like London and Chicago—these same storage and analytic tools could give authorities an unfettered and detailed 24/7 picture of an innocent subject's political and social activities. This suggests that tension in the world of Data 3.0 can be reconciled only through a loosening of what information can be collected and a simultaneous tightening of the standards under which it can be inspected, analyzed, and used.

More specifically with the ongoing evolution of what is private and public, each of the steps of the government intelligence spectrum needs to be revisited and adjusted.

Access ought to be an area in which the government gets relatively wide authority to ensure that it can collect needed and authorized intelligence. But the private sector should not be required to weaken security to facilitate that access.

Requiring companies to build in vulnerabilities would be a strategic mistake, and it would run counter to our democratic values—historically, we have not organized our society to maximize the government's access to communications; instead, we make trade-offs. As I have advocated, "the greater public good is a secure communications infrastructure protected by ubiquitous encryption at the device, server and enterprise level without building in means for government monitoring."[43]

A similar dilemma is posed when the government becomes aware of a preexisting vulnerability that it can exploit for access, but which also entails a structural security weakness that might be exploited by others, including criminals. The NSA, for example, was suspected by some analysts of exploiting a backdoor bug in Juniper Networks routers that potentially weakened encryption, allowing encrypted traffic to be decrypted.[44] More generally, NSA has disclosed that it shares information about the most critical software weaknesses "more than 90 percent of the time."[45] NSA uses the rest of the vulnerabilities to perform its job, or to hold in reserve as "zero days" (flaws that have never yet been used but hold attack potential). In this case, the government is not creating access, but it is also not providing a warning that there is a flaw, resulting in access for itself and possibly others.

Security officials view previously undiscovered security flaws in software as useful in gaining access to adversaries' data for intelligence purposes, but when broadly distributed, security flaws expose individual citizens to security compromise by criminals, terrorists, and even foreign nations.

Where many innocent people might be at risk because of a widespread vulnerability, there is a strong argument for the government to give notice and warn about that vulnerability, even if intelligence officials lose access for espionage purposes. On the other hand, public disclosure may not be necessary if the security flaw exists for only a limited number of subjects, perhaps mostly officials of a hostile government, or if it would be technically difficult for criminals to exploit that flaw.

Of course, the government should be able to resort to its own expertise to build the capabilities to access information on a legally authorized, targeted basis, but it should not require private companies and citizens to design systems deliberately weakened to provide government access. By the same token, there should be a presumption that the government will warn service providers of broadly distributed network or software vulnerabilities.

Collection and Retention

How much restriction ought to be placed on government collection of data of different types is a more debatable question. As noted previously, traditional legal barriers to government surveillance usually attach at the collection phase. Collection of communications is tightly restricted by a judicial warrant requirement in the domestic arena, or in dealing with U.S. citizens. Collection of metadata, as described earlier, is less restricted. Some have argued that even restrictions on metadata collection should be substantially toughened, perhaps by a probable-cause requirement.

In my view, collection of non-content metadata in the arena of national security and cybersecurity—where the aim is to prevent, not prosecute—should be relatively permissive, with no requirement of specific probable cause to believe a crime will be or has been committed. The relevance of specific data to national security is often unclear until well after the opportunity to collect has passed. Once that data is gone, it can never be recovered. Without collection, it's too late to review and analyze. Collection, if guarded against unauthorized review, is not a substantial privacy or autonomy risk.

To be sure, the ability to collect and store data isn't just a remote possibility. The NSA completed its million-square-foot data storage facility in the desert of Bluffdale, Utah, in 2013. This facility was described by Utah governor Gary Herbert as the first in the world with the capability to store a yottabyte (one thousand trillion gigabytes) of data.[46] The NSA itself described the facility as one that "was built with future expansion in mind," making the capability to store data flexible and ever increasing.[47]

Governments need this scale of data to perform their job of protection. But concerns about ensuring only authorized government inspection and use of collected data may be further mitigated if the data is collected and held by private parties, such as telephone or communications providers, and available for review only when a legal threshold is crossed. That is the theory of the recent USA Freedom Act with regard to cell phone metadata. But this approach is practical only if the law requires two elements. First, storage of data by private parties must be mandated for a specified and not limitless time period—say, two years. That way it is available for review when new information comes to light so that analytical conclusions can be drawn. Second, the data should be maintained in a format that is readily searchable by law enforcement or intelligence agencies. If the government obtains a search warrant to collect this data from a third party, such agencies want to be able to read it easily.

A number of European countries have laws governing the retention of data. The French Internal Security Code sets retention periods for data collected, in some cases as short as 30 days.[48] A French national intelligence oversight commission can also recommend halting surveillance activities or destroying collected data.[49] In 2014, Europe's highest court struck down a directive requiring European Union countries to ensure retention of data by telecommunications service providers for between 6 and 24 months. The court reasoned that the directive entailed interference with fundamental rights and that the instruction did not provide sufficient safeguards to limit data retention and protect data collected against abuse.[50] While the time frames specified in these European rulings seem to me impractically short, the principle of a time limit of reasonable duration makes sense.

Inspection, Dissemination, and Action

For access and collection, I propose considerable latitude for government authority, but the actual inspection of collected data (and further dissemination or official action based on that data) is an area in which significant privacy restrictions on government may be needed, even beyond current practice. This was the insight of several justices in the case of *United States v. Jones*: even if government collection of data is currently legally permissible under a very low threshold of relevance—as in streetcam surveillance—the review and use of that data, because of its sheer volume, should be off-limits to government without a warrant. In *Jones*, Justice Samuel Alito emphasized that although the attachment of the GPS to the bottom of Antoine Jones's wife's Jeep was technically a trespass, it was comparatively trivial; what really mattered was the government's *use* of the data.[51] Justice Sonia Sotomayor worried particularly about the government's storing GPS data and "efficiently min[ing] them for years into the future."[52] She therefore suggested that police use of even short-term GPS monitoring might be subject to oversight.[53]

Use of previously collected data is being increasingly constrained. As global mobility of data becomes a constant factor of multinational trade, European views on limiting the use of data are inevitably shaping domestic American rules. In a 2015 legal case, *Schrems v. Data Protection Commissioner*, Europe's top court struck down Safe Harbor, a U.S.-E.U. agreement allowing U.S. companies to self-certify their compliance with E.U. data privacy standards.[54] Maximilian Schrems, an Austrian privacy activist, alleged that Edward

Snowden's unauthorized disclosures revealed the United States provided inadequate privacy protections for E.U. customers' data transferred to the United States. Reasoning that the Safe Harbor arrangement gave the U.S. authorities excessive access to data and provided insufficient means for judicial redress, the court concluded that Safe Harbor interfered with the right to private life under the Charter of Fundamental Rights of the European Union.[55] In February 2016, the United States agreed on a new European Union Privacy Shield framework, requiring U.S. companies to provide stronger protection for the personal data of Europeans.

A step further: there should be additional legal thresholds before certain *types* of predictive analytic tools—including so-called artificial intelligence—can be applied to government-collected data. Artificial intelligence can assemble a detailed analysis of a person's biographical data, generating a behavioral prediction based on that. When the behavioral prediction algorithm actually assigns a risk score to a subject—as in the case of the Fresno police software discussed previously—that calls for additional safeguards. Certainly, there should be limitations on the use of such analysis: mere behavioral prediction alone would not justify restricting these individuals' movement, employment, or free speech.

While we need analytic and predictive tools to be "smarter" at prevention of crime and terror, there should be restrictions based on the level of specificity to which these analytic techniques are applied. So-called microtargeting combines a large number of variables in a quest to predict the behavior, interests, and preferences of *individual* persons. We should have tough restrictions on the government's application of predictive analytic techniques to target individual persons. That said, we should allow the government more leeway to apply predictive analytics to larger, anonymized segments of the population. Of course, even those techniques might be abused to promote racial profiling or other stereotyping.

What We, as Citizens, Should Do to Protect Ourselves

The government should do all it can to protect citizens against online criminals and other hackers, who may seek to steal our identities and money, freeze our computer data to hold it for ransom, and even damage the infrastructure in our houses and automobiles. But we also should take measures to protect ourselves. One of the most devastating cyber incidents ever was the widespread 2017 Wanna-Cry ransomware attack, which exploited a vulnerability in Microsoft's operating system to freeze data in computers across the globe. A month before this occurred, Microsoft circulated a patch to close the vulnerability, which would have prevented the ransomware from entering a network. Sadly, many network operators neglected to download the patch, exposing themselves to a cyber threat that shut down their network operations. For these victims, this cyberattack was utterly avoidable.

Most networks connected to the internet are in private hands. Therefore, unless we invite the government to live in our computers—thereby, eliminating any privacy—we will always be our own first line of defense. Here are some simple tactics that we, as citizens, should adopt to reduce the risks to our own networks and data.

First: Be mindful of what data you transmit and what you connect to your own network.

Every decision to transact online, to furnish sensitive information, or to use publicly available communications infrastructure, such as Wi-Fi, carries with it benefits and risks. The more widely you disseminate sensitive data, the greater the likelihood that it may fall into the wrong hands. Additionally, the more the internet of things expands, the broader the network that can serve as a surface area for attacks. Networked objects are not really smarter—they are just more connected, providing more entry points to your network.

Indeed, for critical physical control systems, you should ask whether your pacemaker is wirelessly connected so it might be hacked.[56] There are now cars in which the steering, drive train, and brakes can be controlled by remote wireless connection. There is value to having these systems connected, but is that convenience worth the risk? If considering buying such an equipped automobile, you should ensure that the manufacturer built into these devices the capability to upgrade security and patch weaknesses so that they are less easily exploitable by hackers.

The truth is that many of these new "smart" connected devices are built with less than minimal security features. They can easily be hacked and turned into a widespread network of remotely controlled zombies: a botnet. In a 2016 incident, printers, cameras, baby monitors, and similar devices attached to the DNS service provider Dyn were infected with Marai malware. Remotely directed to generate an excessive volume of traffic, Dyn was overwhelmed. Internet users were shut out of numerous websites for many hours. In this case, innocent internet users—and many brand-name businesses—suffered the consequences of inadequate security built into millions of simple home devices. To protect your data, and to avoid allowing your device to be hijacked into becoming part of a destructive botnet, the lesson is to buy only connected devices that allow security updates.

Second: Practice cyber hygiene.

That means taking basic precautions. Avoid simple or obvious passwords, or passwords that can be guessed by researching your biography, such as your mother's maiden name. Change your passwords periodically, and don't use the same password for all your data fields or internet sites. If you are emailing a password-protected document, do not also email the password. Send it by text or telephone. Use multifaceted authentication of identity where available, or confirm the legitimacy of a transaction by insisting on verification by telephone or text.

Third: Take advantage of cybersecurity technology.

Reputable service providers frequently update operating systems to correct vulnerabilities or flaws, or to build defenses against newly discovered malicious exploits, viruses, or worms. Be sure to update virus protections or to download software updates that plug or remedy vulnerabilities in your computer.

The best defense is a layered defense—one that detects and resolves an attack by protecting the network's data at multiple levels. Many people think that security lives only at the perimeter and that defense is keeping malware totally out. But the reality is that some malware will penetrate even a defended perimeter and will enter the network. Usually, the real damage occurs the longer the intruder remains within your network. A hacker can use the initial stages of penetration to scout your network, determine what is of value, set up a communications link back to a control server off-site, and steal credentials that can be used to open individual compartments within your network.

Obviously, a strong perimeter defense is crucial, but it is just as important to set up defenses *within* your network, especially with respect to your most sensitive data. This is achieved by segmenting your data within the network: setting up compartments for your most valuable data and requiring further authentication to access it. Continuous diagnosis and monitoring of what occurs within your network are key, as these measures inform you if someone is trying to access or move sensitive data in a suspicious manner. Recent developments in behavioral analytics allow computer systems themselves to detect anomalous behavior and to raise a red flag.

Finally, developments in biometric—fingerprint, facial, or iris—identification and in the encryption of data itself are important security enablers. Encrypted data, even if stolen, is useless without the decryption key. We need to use encryption tools and consider supplementing password requirements with another form of identity authentication, such as a fingerprint or iris scan.

One way to think of the architecture of a secure cyber network is to consider the most agile defense system in the world: the human body. Our bodies are designed with strong external defenses against bacteria and viruses. But these do not screen out everything. Our immune system is the next line of defense; when something foreign enters our bodies, a healthy immune system characterizes it, and if it's a threat, our white blood cells will kill it. In a way, immunization is a form of threat-information-sharing with our immune system: our annual flu vaccine tells white blood cells the "signature" of the current flu virus so our bodies can detect and kill the real intruder.

Fourth: Don't be fooled.

Many data hacks are carried out not by brilliant circumvention of software defenses, but by simple trickery—fooling a user into downloading a malicious tool or a virus by visiting a counterfeit website or clicking on a phony link embedded in an email. The latter technique, known as phishing, relies on tricking the recipient of an email into clicking on an enclosed attachment with malicious computer code concealed within. Many of these emails are artfully designed to appear genuine. Skilled hackers may research your online persona so the email can appear to be from a real friend referencing a real event. The days when online frauds were all perpetrated by obvious phonies using broken English or advancing ridiculous pleas for money from a foreign prince are long gone.

When in doubt about a link, seek an out of band confirmation—like a text or a phone call—to verify that the email and link are genuine. A responsive email is not sufficient, since the scammer may be using a stolen identity credential from your real friend. Much better proof of genuineness is a personal conversation or a reference in the transmitting email that relates to an event or discussion known only to the sender and you.

CHAPTER FIVE

DATA 3.0 AND CONTROLS ON PRIVATE SECTOR USE OF DATA

Private parties may make use of collected data for many purposes. This chapter considers limits on private companies that make big data analytics the centerpiece of their business model. While I have called for adjusting the restrictions on government storage, use, and analysis of collected data, I also think the private sector should not have unfettered ability to exploit and sell that same information.

Do Service Providers Ever Have a Duty to Police the Networks They Maintain?

Putting aside the rules controlling when government can review and analyze collected data, we must also determine when or if it is appropriate to impose on private service providers the obligation to scrutinize traffic they host for (1) impermissible content, like child porn; (2) recruitment for or precursors to acts of terrorism or violence, such as a social media post indicating the intent to carry out an attack; or (3) malicious tools or viruses that are designed to directly compromise or interfere with data networks. There are networks and platforms that have no ability to inspect the traffic they host, and others that do have such ability. The latter platforms will examine traffic to target users with ads or to aggregate user data for other reasons. But that same capability allows them to edit or restrict malicious content.

In such cases, there is considerable force to the argument that the service provider should take steps to block injurious content or warn government authorities to prevent violence or abuse. By analogy, medical ethics require providers to breach confidentiality if a patient expresses the intent to commit an act of violence against another, and some laws also recognize these obligations. For instance, in *Tarasoff v. Regents of the University of California*, a male student confided to a psychotherapist his fantasies of killing a female classmate; two months later, he stabbed her to death. The California supreme court held that therapists who learn that their patients pose a serious threat of violence have a duty to exercise reasonable care to protect foreseeable victims.[1] The laws of various states recognize similar duties; but in resolving the competing interests in protecting people from violence and promoting patient-therapist confidentiality and care, the laws differ about liability, the specificity of the threat, and the duty to warn potential victims or to protect them by hospitalizing patients.[2]

But, importantly, restrictions on communication that endorses violence should be applied carefully to avoid shutting down speech that may be obnoxious but is not actually inciting violence. For example, on October 13, 2015, Richard Lakin was fatally wounded in an attack on a bus in Jerusalem. His family reportedly later learned that one of the attackers had announced his attack plans on Facebook. Consequently, a group of 20,000 Israelis sued Facebook in New York State trial court "to stop allowing Palestinian terrorists to incite violent attacks against Israeli citizens on its internet platform." Another group of plaintiffs also sued as the estates of U.S. citizens who had been killed by terrorist attacks.[3] The complaints alleged that Facebook was complicit in Lakin's death, as well as a wave of attacks on Jewish Israelis, because the attackers read hateful posts on Facebook that incited them to murder and glorified violence, and because Facebook is not a neutral party—its algorithms allegedly help the inciters find people sympathetic to their cause by offering friend, group, and event suggestions based on users' "likes" and browsing history. The lawsuits sought an injunction requiring the internet giant to monitor its platform for posts inciting violence, to take down such posts, and to change its policies accordingly.[4]

The plaintiffs argued for an injunction in part on the basis of Israeli law, which penalizes the publication of praise, support, or calls for support of terrorism or its incitement. As Professor Eugene Volokh has written, enforcing such a prohibition would violate the First Amendment to the U.S. Constitution. It would restrict a large category of permissible speech; it would be overbroad.[5] Even if a court considered only the plaintiffs' more limited demand for Facebook to "immediately remove all pages, groups and posts containing incitement to murder Jews," under U.S. law, constitutionally unprotected "incitement" is only speech that incites "imminent" criminal conduct—violence that is about to happen, not violence at some undefined future time. That would exclude many of the incidents listed in the complaints. Further, a congressional statute, Section 230 of the Communications Decency Act, broadly protects internet service providers from civil liability for content their users post.[6] In short, the government does not require these companies to censor their users' content, even if it's hateful, obscene, defamatory, or constitutionally unprotected.

After the lawsuits were transferred to federal court, they were dismissed on a variety of grounds including the Communications Decency Act. But the lawsuits demonstrate that people are increasingly asserting the obligations of internet service providers to police their networks. Similarly, United States and European officials have asserted that internet media platforms should shut down sites whose users recruit terrorists or incite violence. Facebook, Google, Yahoo, and other internet companies remove thousands of pieces of content from their platforms every month through internal policies or procedures. Most of these decisions do not see the light of day, and few become fodder for litigation, although some ejected users have complained that their free speech is being violated. In fact, section 230 in the Decency Act also immunizes service providers in taking good faith actions to restrict access to speech that is "obscene," "excessively violent," "harassing," "or otherwise objectionable [in] content," even if such content is normally constitutionally protected.[7]

Beyond removing clearly objectionable material, there is the more complicated question of how to deal with online advocacy by extremist groups of all types: Islamist, neo-Nazi, or extreme anarchists. That advocacy may not rise to the level of incitement or recruitment, but it could serve as a gateway to both. There are those who believe such advocacy should be suppressed, and internet companies have increasingly heeded these calls, especially after the violent demonstrations in August 2017 by white supremacists in Charlottesville, Virginia.

We should be careful about an overly broad approach. First, it places social media service providers in the role of arbiters or editors of content. That runs counter to the existing model that treats these providers as neutral transmitters of content and insulates them from legal responsibility and from liability for injurious content. If social media companies become more deeply engaged in value judgments about what is permitted content, their neutrality and even their credibility may be drawn into question. Then media platforms may be viewed as electronically responsible for all the content they host. Equally important is that with an open internet (rather than a bounded internet, as in China), efforts to suppress advocacy on social media will drive extremists to new sites, perhaps on the dark web. After Charlottesville, removal of certain extremist accounts from mainstream social media companies led to the movement of net traffic to Gab, a site that did not inhibit so-called alt-right content.[8]

A more promising strategy may be the one adopted by Jigsaw, an affiliate of Google. Rather than shut down extremist sites, Google monitors them and presents visitors to those sites with prominent links to sites that provide balanced or contrary material. In effect, the same technique used to generate commercial advertisements relevant to online searchers is adapted to provide counter-extremist material to those searching extremist sites. This approach has two advantages: it honors the principle of uncensored content while it combats extremism more effectively than the more overt approach of outright suppression.[9]

How Do We Address "Fake News"?

Even more complicated are the issues raised by recent calls for media platforms to restrict or block so-called fake news. The concepts of propaganda and deceptive-information operations date back many centuries, and the former Soviet Union and its affiliated network of the Communist International were notable for their efforts to propagate false news stories as a geopolitical tool. Until recently, however, the reach of such information operations was limited. Falsified stories had to circulate using relatively marginal communications media, like posters, newsletters, or government-operated newspapers and broadcasters. Or the mainstream media had to be fooled into publishing falsehoods.

The rise of internet platforms democratized mass communication and, thus, significantly scaled up the opportunity to distribute falsehoods. Not only can anybody connected to the internet use Twitter, blogging, and social media to publish stories globally, but also it is relatively easy to use anonymity or even impersonation to disguise the fact that the propagator is a terrorist network or a nation-state and its agents. Moreover, communication technology facilitates techniques such as altering photographs or creating phony documents.

Of course, posting falsehoods online by no means guarantees that they will be widely read. Any posting must compete with millions of other circulating items. But certain features of the internet can facilitate a determined effort to drive actual readership through "false amplification."[10] For example, automated botnets or teams of government agents can drive readership by artificially increasing the number of "clicks" of a false story, thus stimulating its standing in search engines that measure trending stories. Hackers can impersonate individuals on social media networks and send phony stories to "friends," creating a false sense of validation. By relentlessly generating trending stories or false "friend recommendations," fake stories that would normally receive little notice dramatically expand their reach.

As fake news has expanded in scale, its impact on politics has become notable. Those studying Russian efforts to influence and even subvert public opinion in Europe have observed the increase in internet-driven fake news over the last several years. Russian military thinking expressly notes that efforts to undermine public confidence in governments through information operations like false news are a powerful tool in geopolitical competition.[11]

These efforts have had real impact—influencing, for example, Central European populations to adopt a more skeptical attitude toward the West and the E.U. as compared with their attitude toward Russia. More significant is the effect of this disinformation campaign in undermining trust in traditional news sources and professional media.[12] And for the first time, the 2016 U.S. presidential campaign highlighted the effects of fake news on American political processes.

Not surprisingly, there has been increasing discussion about combating or limiting fake news.[13] In 2017, the German Bundestag passed a law authorizing fines for social networks that do not remove "fake news."[14] Ironically, Russian officials have long argued that cybersecurity should be understood to encompass restrictions on "harmful" information.[15] That underscores the danger in overregulating in this area; the Russian government views "fake news" as information that is disagreeable to government policy. And recent history has shown how even American politicians have rushed to embrace the term "fake news" to characterize criticism or unpleasant news stories.

While the dangers of fake news are real, direct regulation of content would be a cure worse than the disease. Putting aside outright forgeries or concocted photographs, evaluation of the accuracy of content is often fuzzy, particularly when controversy centers on the causes of an event, or what inferences should be drawn from a particular set of facts. Regulation of content itself is inherently subject to manipulation, especially when government overseers have a vested interest that colors their perspectives.

That's not to say nothing should be done. If we turn from false content to false amplification, a number of approaches would mitigate much of the harm caused by these disinformation operations—and without infringing on free speech. For example, detection and suppression of botnets or of concerted campaigns to artificially drive trending on search engines are a content-neutral way to limit information campaigns. Even more compelling is a requirement that impersonators on social media be unmasked, so falsehoods cannot be promoted through the pretense that these are legitimate recommendations of one's friends or even of celebrities and other public figures.

As the internet increasingly becomes a medium for terrorist recruitments, incitement of violence, and even automated manipulation of public opinion, our policymakers and technologists must work together to clarify the rules of the road. Internet service providers have both the obligation and the capability to monitor the traffic they host, but blocking traffic should be carefully limited to clear recruitment by those intending to incite others to violence. At the same time, providers can and should block automated online campaigns to influence search engines, as well as the use of false identities or impersonation to drive news stories.

Should There Be Limits on What Service Providers Can Do with Digital Exhaust?

According to security expert Bruce Schneier, "by 2010, we as a species were creating more data per day than we did from the beginning of time until 2003."[16] The scope of private collection is rapidly expanding. With the advent of the cloud, the private sector has far surpassed the government's ability to collect and use data. These capabilities include the following:

- Social media
- Location, GPS, and cell information
- Search-engine results
- Tracking purchases
- Uploading fitness and other personal data

To an even greater extent than the police predictive software discussed earlier, this consumer data provides an almost complete picture of someone's behavior, activities, and beliefs. The same tools previously identified for police monitoring can be modified for reviewing information to extract preferences.

A Stanford University study utilized the phone metadata of volunteers to understand how much information is contained in today's digital exhaust. Based only on the phone metadata, the researchers were able determine that "Participant A" made phone calls to specialty pharmacies and neurology groups for relapsing multiple sclerosis. "Participant B" spoke at length with cardiologists and placed phone calls to a hotline for monitoring cardiac arrhythmia. "Participant C" made phone calls to a firearm store specializing in semiautomatic rifles. The person also spoke with firearm customer service. "Participant D" contacted "a home improvement store, locksmiths, a hydroponics dealer, and a head shop." "Participant E" had a long conversation with her sister, followed up by several phone calls to Planned Parenthood. These were followed up by phone calls to Planned Parenthood two weeks and one month later.[17]

Obvious conclusions from the study can be drawn regarding a multiple sclerosis sufferer, a heart condition patient, a firearm enthusiast, a marijuana farmer, and a person choosing to have an abortion. The suspected heart condition patient and the firearm enthusiast were later confirmed by the research team with other public information sources. The other conditions were not further investigated for confirmation, given privacy sensitivities.

The more data that is collected and aggregated, the more a person's habits, preferences, beliefs, and actions can be monitored, predicted, and even shaped. Collection of this information is often not illegal, but the amount of information it yields may be "creepy" and discomforting. We haven't yet developed human intuition regarding what counts as an invasion of privacy from data sources in the same way that we have developed it for "real world" experiences. Privacy allows for distance from monitoring so that we can exercise free expression. It prevents us from being manipulated. Privacy secures our freedom.

Once collected, this information is almost unlimited in terms of storage and use. It is often aggregated and sold. It may be used to enhance online services, but, as previously described, it may also be used to market products, evaluate job applicants, set insurance rates, and even set pricing for certain services.

Meaningful Consent

Most data harvesters rest their authority on consent by the subscribers or users—who often click their acceptance of lengthy and verbose terms of service. But aside from explicit consent or the voluntary submission of data to social media, there are many more avenues of collection.

In an age of big data, individuals leave a digital footprint almost wherever they go and whatever they do online. Many daily activities yield data elements that are obtained without explicit consent or even knowledge by the subject. For example, retail discount cards may be offered without a clear statement about the end use of the data. Location signals from mobile phones—necessary for proper functioning—also generate information that the user may not understand or agree to, or about which there is no realistic option to consent because that data is an intrinsic by-product of the functioning of the device. People rarely understand or give knowledgeable consent to having this data reviewed, sold, and used elsewhere.

Company arrangements with third parties mean that personal data can be disseminated without individual knowledge or meaningful consent. Individuals who do not consent even implicitly may have their data uploaded anyway. For example, if photos of a third person are taken or activities of a passerby are recorded, these may be uploaded and aggregated not just to the individual photographer's device, but to a cloud-based service. The cloud service provider could, in theory, aggregate all data collected from all sources about the same individual subject without the knowledge or permission of the person being photographed or recorded. Thus, a celebrity or public figure who did not utilize the service provider and who did not consent could still generate a significant personal profile for the service provider to use or market.

The advent of the internet of things will further expand the volume and sensitivity of data generated about essentially unwitting individuals.

If we adapt the continuum model applied earlier in the context of government surveillance, should there be restrictions on collection, analysis, use, retention, and dissemination? Much of this will be a function of what threshold of warning and explicitness should be set for consent to be found.

There are two ways that collected data can be used. One is to improve the functionality of the application or feature, such as using locational data for Google Maps. I call this intrinsic use of the data. Arguably another example is using purchase history to recommend new purchases, à la Amazon, or even to facilitate monitoring inventory at a retail establishment. But data can also be marketed to third parties, and used not only to facilitate advertising but also to assess behavior that might be of interest to a wide variety of businesses for employment, pricing, or insurance decisions: extrinsic use of the data. For example, a prospective employer could be interested in assessing the totality of data about an applicant's spending, exercising, reading, and exercise habits.

This suggests the threshold for consent should be different for intrinsic use by the data collector and extrinsic use by a third party that buys data or seeks to aggregate multiple data streams. Perhaps for intrinsic use it ought to be presumed that the user of a feature wants that functionality to improve. But for extrinsic uses by third parties like marketers, clear notice and explicit affirmative consent should be required. This is particularly true when data is bought, sold, or aggregated from multiple sources, which may provide a much richer picture of individuals' behavior than they imagine. This issue will intensify as more objects become data sources in the internet of things.

An additional question arises about what happens when non-subscriber data is swept up by private companies and used for their own purposes. As described above, the advent of cloud computing meant that a single service provider could host data for thousands, even millions, of individual subscriber accounts. If a service provider can search across all these accounts, considerable data about even a nonuser third party can be developed and utilized. This may flow from a particular individual, such as a public figure, being photographed or recorded by many subscribers on their own social and other media, or by data generated through private video. There are two distinct consent questions. First, did the photographer or creator of the record consent to its use or redistribution? That question essentially mirrors the issue whenever a data generator must consent to use by a service provider. But an additional question is: When is consent needed from the non-subscriber, who is also perhaps the unwitting subject of the data recording?

Normally, if one photographs or records activity in a public space, the person being photographed has no right to control the data. No one asks a third-party subject about consent, other than as a matter of politeness. But if a service provider can aggregate a trove of this data from individual recorders who are all storing it in the cloud, that aggregation requires limitations, or an additional level of consent by the subject. This is a variation of the same issue that the courts have considered in the context of ubiquitous government surveillance in public spaces. There should be constraints on how such data may be aggregated and used, much as government surveillance even in public spaces is now being restricted.[18] For example, if an insurance company harvests non-subscriber data from a variety of sources, it should not be able to use that data without notice to and consent by the data subject.

Setting Limits on Data Use

Currently, there are few absolute limits on what private companies can do with big data, or when it can be shared with other companies. Recent legislative and regulatory efforts in the United States to limit these uses have not progressed; in Europe, by contrast, use and resale of data are closely regulated.

Recall the near-future fictional scenario of James at the beginning of this book. Through 24-hour monitoring—including measuring of food intake, timing of hours of rest, and daily blood and urine sampling—a treasure trove of information can be created for the benefit of private companies. For example, health insurers interested in driving down insurance costs can motivate insured individuals toward healthier lifestyles. By encouraging policyholders' healthier eating, sleeping, and exercise habits, the companies increase their profit margins. Employers determined to prevent litigation and to increase productivity could also encourage approved off-hour behavior. By tracking its workers' off-hour locations, and urging proper rest, an employer could help ensure its employees remain out of trouble and return maximum benefit toward corporate interests. Big Brother (or Big Nanny), here we come.

Less obviously intrusive uses of such data have already begun. As described, several auto insurers currently offer a discount to drivers who embed in their car a device that records their driving habits. The argument is that this device provides a more accurate assessment of risk and allows safe drivers to get the benefit of their behavior. Health insurers are beginning to do the same thing with activity monitors worn by individuals. Options for tracking meals are usually provided as a convenience with the tracking software.

Obviously, there are direct benefits to the individual involved in these situations: increased safety during travel and a healthier body. However, we frequently trade away our data for a short-term convenience or lower-cost gratification without realizing the long-term consequences. It's certainly unnerving to realize we have no idea how our data might be used, nor by whom, nor for what. Imagine your health insurer purchasing records of your restaurant and grocery store purchases to determine what kind of foods you eat. What consent should be required for that?

There are also instances in which insurers could say that if you do not consent to comprehensive monitoring of your lifestyle (via data), you will be charged the highest premium rate, or even worse, denied insurance altogether. Already, as mentioned earlier, certain prospective employers are skeptical about candidates who do not use social media—speculating that they have something to hide. Why don't they have an online presence that is easily viewable and can be used to determine their behaviors and make assumptions about their character? If it means anything, our right to privacy and autonomy should encompass the right to opt out of generating the data stream.

Finally, the full implications of ubiquitous data collection are often unclear even to sophisticated users. For example, a smartphone owner using a mapping application must reveal her location to the app to use it. Because her data may be valuable to pattern software, the app provider is incentivized to hold on to her information. By default, this individual's data is not protected.

The Waze traffic application on numerous phones is a tremendously convenient navigation tool. Perhaps the most effective and powerful direction-finding tool, Waze gathers data from thousands of users and applies its algorithms to determine the locations of accidents, traffic slowdowns, and other navigation issues. This tool saves valuable time for drivers by allowing them to avoid congested areas and locate new paths to destinations. Unbeknownst to most users, however, in its default setting, the Waze application never stops tracking phones' locations. Only users who pay sufficient attention and understand background settings are able to disable the constant tracking.[19] This continual tracking makes perfect sense if you are the Waze algorithm developer. More data allows for better understanding. By even more effectively predicting navigation hot spots, it also results in a better product for the user.

But there is a downside: the convenience also allows for others to stalk you. Researchers from the University of California at Santa Barbara have shown that by manipulation of the data stream through virtual armies of "ghost vehicles," individual users can be tracked and manipulated.[20]

Users of the Waze application can also identify police vehicles for others logged on to the application. Seemingly innocuous as a warning to prevent getting caught in a speed trap, this data can be used to track the police. Because the user does not know whether the officers are actually in a speed trap or just stopped for lunch, identifying their location to bad actors potentially puts officers at risk. Law enforcement officials have recently expressed concern about the app after two New York Police Department officers were killed at the end of 2014 by a man who had been using Waze for months to track officers.[21]

The convenience of a few minutes of saved time seems a poor trade for the safety of police officers or a loss of privacy. But users are lured by short-term convenience, and few have consciously made this trade-off. Some may trust that the data exchanged will be used only for good causes. However, what is "good" differs among individuals, companies, and the public. In an age of competing interests, the defaults are changing.

A Right to Be Forgotten

A distinct issue is raised when third-party collection is undertaken by, or obtained by, the news media. Since the subject of the data is not the generator of the data, there is no obvious ownership right by the data subject. Western democracies do not normally require consent when the press and similar institutions collect or publish information about third parties, provided that it is true and not a violation of copyright law. But European countries, which, as we have seen, place much heavier emphasis on data privacy than the United States does, increasingly have formulated a "right to be forgotten." A data subject may petition authorities to require search engines to delete links to personal information that, while truthful, is nevertheless deemed irrelevant because of age, context, or some other sensitivity.

In 2010, a Spanish citizen filed a complaint with a Spanish data protection agency complaining that an online search of his name brought up an old news story from 1998 that his property was being sold to cover social security debts.[22] He argued that these attachment proceedings had been resolved and were no longer relevant. Therefore, both a Spanish newspaper and Google should be required to remove or conceal the information.[23] The data protection agency denied the request against the newspaper; that information was lawfully published, pursuant to a government order to publicize the auction widely.[24] But Google was different; the agency found that Google was a "data controller." Under a European Union directive on privacy protections for handling personal information, Google had to change its search results.[25]

A higher E.U. court ruled that individuals may petition to have personal information that is "inadequate, irrelevant or no longer relevant, or excessive in relation to [the] purposes of data processing" removed from search engines, and that search engines must delete those links absent the "preponderant interest of the general public" in having access to the information.[26]

In the two years following the May 2014 ruling by Europe's top court, Google received 407,673 requests to remove personal information from its search results. It has evaluated 1,425,748 URLs, removing 516,575, or 42.6 percent of them.[27] Among the requests—performer Axl Rose demanding that Google remove unflattering photographs.[28]

To be sure—absurd cases aside—the European ruling has intuitive appeal. For instance, victims of rape and other crimes have been able to get search results on such stories unlisted to protect their identities. But the decision has generated considerable criticism; by privileging privacy too much, the right to be forgotten threatens to restrict freedom of speech and public access to true information.

Toward a Solution: A Framework for Use of Data

In the search for a solution to the issues of third-party collection, the basic rights of privacy and, more broadly, autonomy must never be forgotten or ignored. From the standpoint of free speech and democratic values, a framework should allow news organizations and individual citizens to collect and use data that is either recorded by them, or obtained with the consent of the data subject from third-party collectors. That would be particularly true for data about public figures. Individuals in public office have long been held to a reduced legal right to object to public discourse about themselves. Because in their elected office they represent public good, the media is given liberty in accessing and presenting collected information about elected officials.

For commercially acquired non-media-related data— recognizing that in American jurisprudence, commercial speech is accorded less protection than political or artistic communication—the rules should be different. As suggested previously, for user data collected to improve the functionality of the user experience, consent should be presumed. This would be the case, for example, if locational data is collected to improve the accuracy of a map application. But for user data collected for other commercial purposes, such as marketing products, the user should be asked to opt in affirmatively; in some instances, perhaps, compensation might be offered as an inducement. Finally, before aggregated nonuser data can be used commercially for a purpose other than what was originally approved, the subject should be notified and specifically asked *to opt in or opt out* of the change in use. These rules will allow commercial enterprises to harness the benefits of big data but will also respect the principles of individual liberty and privacy.

Opting in or out of data sharing should be a meaningful choice, not one that is compelled. Where a service provider has monopoly power over a service, consent to unrestricted use of data should not be a condition for participation. As providers assume market-leading positions, it is appropriate to limit the breadth of the data uses for which they seek consent. And employers and insurers should be reasonably limited in the breadth of data to which they demand access as a condition of employment or insurance.

The United States should also adopt a limited version of the European right to be forgotten. This right has historically been implied by the limited human ability to retain information and the fact that even recorded information (such as photographs) would both be generally limited in dissemination and deteriorate over time. Modern data tools no longer allow this to happen naturally. The rights of people to be excluded from search under conventional search tools might be most advantageous to minors and private individuals; on the other hand, public figures should have no right to be excluded from online searching. The availability of such a right of search exclusion should depend upon the nature of the data in question and the purposes for which a search might occur, and by whom. Yet an additional question—both practical and legal—is whether a right to be forgotten extends beyond search tools and might actually mandate erasure from databases. This would occur in the same way that social media sites block and eliminate child pornography today. However, extending a right to erase entries from underlying databases goes too far, and smacks uncomfortably of literally rewriting history, as in George Orwell's *1984*.

What We, as Citizens, Should Do to Better Control Our Data

Our control over our personal data is largely dependent on choices we make. Under any set of rules about consent, it is our responsibility to make deliberate choices when agreeing to the use of our data. That means asking what benefits are to be gained in granting consent, or how our data might be used. What's the trade-off?

For example, often a newly downloaded application asks whether we agree to share our locational data "for better service." Locational data, once harvested and stored, can yield a granular picture of our daily activities, especially when combined with other data. So we must ask how sharing our data yields better service *for us*. With GPS-mapping applications, the benefit is clear. For retail establishments, it is less obvious how we benefit from their pinpointing our location, unless it is to target us with more precise advertising.

By the same token, it is worth being conscious about our online searches. They often leave digital footprints. If we persistently search for illness symptoms, an insurer might someday inquire why we were so interested. Logging on to a controversial website could also attract misguided or unwelcome attention. In 2017, the Department of Justice sought data from a website called DreamHost, which was used to organize protests during the 2017 presidential inauguration. The warrant was so broad as to call for the IP address of any visitor to the site, estimated at a total of roughly 1.3 million addresses.[29] Even a curiosity seeker would be swept up by this government inquiry.

One suggestion: sensitive searches might be undertaken not on one's own device, but at a library or another venue with a publicly available log-on address.

Internet service providers and platforms provide convenience, service, and benefit, but the best way to control our data is to be mindful of how and when we generate it. As the traditional internet saying goes, if the service is "free," you are probably the product.

CHAPTER SIX

DATA 3.0 AND SOVEREIGNTY: A QUESTION OF CONFLICT OF LAWS

With data effortlessly crossing borders, law and government policy take on another dimension. In a global world, it's difficult to determine whose rules to follow.

Data in Motion and Data at Rest

By definition, the internet is ubiquitous, and data flows globally. In reality, data must be housed on physical infrastructure and move through routers and over fiber-optic or wireless transmission technology. The question arises as to whose rules apply, and if the location of the infrastructure becomes the guiding principle. This would have the perverse effect of nations either demanding or creating incentives to house servers locally, or in countries with laws most favorable to internet service providers. If each nation demands that data pertaining to its own citizens is stored within its own borders, this could give rise to a fragmentation of the internet. That sort of Balkanization would most certainly lead to engineering inefficiencies and, worse yet, an internet full of gaps and seams.

As an example, Facebook is designed in a way that maximizes availability, scalability, and retention of the data it collects. The company's data is physically stored in many locations to ensure that it is always available, with backups that are regularly checked. Consequently, it may prove difficult to determine at any one time where a specific "piece" of data exists, and once it is deleted by the user, whether all copies of this data are removed.[1]

However, if we apply the traditional U.S. legal view that any transaction touching the United States is subject to U.S. law, then almost every country with a developed communications infrastructure can claim legal jurisdiction over internet data. First, information packets may move through many countries before they reach their destination. This is compounded by wireless networks—imagine an individual flying across Europe while emailing or downloading a news feed. In theory, every country in the flight path could claim jurisdiction.

We are left with two questions—one regarding the legal process for access to data, and the other the substantive decision about what nation's laws govern the handling of data that lives outside the physical realm of borders.

Law Enforcement Access to Data

With data at rest in servers or in motion across borders, there may be conflicting demands for lawful access to it, under possibly incompatible legal rules. This issue has arisen in legal cases in which data resides in servers in one country but is requested by another country where the data creator is a citizen. The complexity may be further compounded when the internet service provider is a corporate citizen of a third nation but does business in all three. There are procedural questions regarding whether legal process can be served directly on the internet service provider, but also whether such requests should be channeled through various treaty mechanisms.

The issue is not theoretical. In December 2013, the U.S. government served a search warrant on Microsoft, seeking emails and other private information associated with a particular customer account as part of a criminal narcotics investigation. Microsoft's Global Criminal Compliance team discovered that some of the information resided on U.S. servers but that the emails associated with the account were stored on Microsoft's servers in Dublin, Ireland. Microsoft turned over the information stored in the United States but refused to comply with the request to hand over the information stored abroad.[2]

The district court affirmed a magistrate judge's order, holding that a warrant issued pursuant to the Stored Communications Act (SCA) requires a U.S. internet service provider to produce emails stored on a foreign server.[3] When

Microsoft refused to comply with the order, the judge found the company in contempt of court. Microsoft appealed the ruling, and the order was reversed by the U.S. Court of Appeals for the Second Circuit. That court held that because the data was held in servers in Ireland, the statutory authority to issue the warrant was lacking.[4] In 2018, the case was to be decided by the U.S. Supreme Court.

Much of the legal argument turns on interpretation of the SCA, a statute written in 1986, well before widespread public adoption of the internet. Microsoft argued that the warrant cannot be executed outside the United States; courts typically presume that statutes do not apply extraterritorially. Microsoft also said that the U.S. government must instead work through its mutual legal assistance treaty with Ireland and other diplomatic channels to obtain the data.

In reaching its decision in *Microsoft*, the appellate court weighed two factors. First, the country with jurisdiction over the physical data center generally has its own data privacy rules. Second, one nation's desire to seize an individual's data physically stored in overseas servers circumvents the (admittedly cumbersome) treaty process through which sovereign nations share evidence. But one factor to which the court gave no weight was the citizenship or location of the actual person owning the data on Microsoft's Dublin server. One might reasonably think this the weightiest factor in evaluating the privacy interests involved.

Both parties agreed that the U.S. Congress needs to update existing congressional statutes to meet the realities of global electronic communications. United States lawmakers have introduced several bills to do just that. The

International Communications Privacy Act (ICPA) and the Email Privacy Act would require law enforcement to get warrants for data stored for longer than 180 days. ICPA and the CLOUD act of 2018 would also limit the extraterritorial reach of search warrants for stored data.[5]

Law enforcement access to data located abroad has been a problem for other countries, too. In 2016, as part of a drug trafficking investigation, a Brazilian judge asked Facebook to provide information on an account on WhatsApp, a messaging service acquired by Facebook. After the company reportedly refused several times to comply, Brazil's federal police arrested a Facebook executive.[6]

What National Laws Govern Rights and Responsibilities for Data That May Be Stored Anyplace?

Laws governing data are contradictory around the world, though some countries seek to impose their views concerning permissible communication and privacy upon actors whose only contact with those countries is the happenstance of where their data is stored or sent.

The European Court of Justice recently ruled that because data privacy laws in the United States are not as restrictive as those in the European Union, transnational enterprises may not be able to transfer any information relating to European citizens to databases in the United States.[7] This would apply to the most mundane and routine internal business data about employees, such as payroll or accrued leave, or even business-travel information. New rules promulgated in the E.U. under its General Data Protection Regulation impose penalties on any data controller or service provider in any country that manages personal data of any E.U. citizen if that controller or provider does not obey European privacy rules. As of spring 2018, when the new rule was to become effective, the GDPR would have the effect of either requiring all data relating to Europeans to be housed separately in Europe, or—the more likely intent—the de facto spreading of Europe's privacy regulatory footprint into the United States. It would be easier for America to comply with a tougher standard for everyone than to create a separate regime just for European data. Perhaps the issue seems benign and easily resolved by non-European nations embracing Europe's tougher privacy laws. But if those laws unduly hamper law enforcement or security, there could be a cost. This is an example of conflicting government legal regimes fragmenting the rules of data handling in a global information environment.

Even thornier is the situation when one nation's expansion of privacy rights directly collides with another's free speech rights. For example, consider Europe's "right to be forgotten" law, under which the subject of a story accessible through a search engine on the internet could demand that web links to the story be removed because the story invades privacy. This ruling was not limited to proven falsehoods, or stories or images involving children or victims of crime. Among the items that have been deleted from search engines are a Wikipedia page,[8] a story about an informal Post-it note art competition, news articles about a former soccer referee who lied about calls he made on the field, and a BBC article about a Merrill Lynch executive blamed for helping to bring about the financial crisis.[9]

Initially, global search companies responded to the European right-to-be-forgotten rule by dropping search links from European sites but not from sites housed in the United States. (Most searches are conducted on country-specific sites.) But in a practical sense this resulted in incomplete compliance because determined searchers could connect to a non-European site to conduct their search. Accordingly, French authorities mandated that "forgetfulness" apply to all sites operated by the search engine, as long as the search-engine company was present in some sense in Europe. Google initially resisted this move. At one time, the company encouraged online users to search using the U.S. domain name (google .com) as opposed to domain names in Europe (for example, google.de or google.co.uk). However, Google recently announced that, as part of its implementation of the right-to-be-forgotten rule, searches conducted on browsers within the European Union will now be blocked from searching for "forgotten" data on all domain names worldwide.[10]

That expansion of a singular view of privacy collides with American free-speech rights. If a European court sought to enforce a right to be forgotten in the United States, one can easily envision a U.S. court forbidding that enforcement. The same effect could occur under European rules barring speech that disparages ethnic groups and (as discussed above) "fake news," or under rules from nations that bar politically unpopular speech or religious blasphemy. Moreover, Latin American nations are now beginning to assert similar claims to take down material from the internet, and it is not hard to envision that Chinese and Russian regulators might have their own views of what should be forgotten.

Choice-of-Law Rules: Some Alternatives

Our current situation is unsustainable. As the internet enables more and more transactions, disputes arising from those transactions are multiplying rapidly. In resolving these disputes, it matters very much whose law governs. Some countries are moving to require companies to keep data about their own citizens on physical infrastructure within the country—so-called data localization laws. Other countries are writing laws that apply extraterritorially.

With my colleague Paul Rosenzweig, I have argued elsewhere that the current free-for-all must yield to an international choice-of-law framework.[11] Several approaches exist. A choice-of-law rule could be based on (1) the citizenship of the data creator; (2) the citizenship of the data subject; (3) the citizenship of the data holder; or (4) the location of the harm.

To understand how each of these rules would work in practice, imagine a dispute over a work of art. The photographer (the data creator) takes a picture of a woman (the data subject). The photographer and the woman are citizens of different countries—Finland and Sweden, for example. Without the woman's consent, the photographer stores the photograph on a server in Ireland (the data holder). The server is hacked and the data is seized by a Vietnamese company that reproduces it for advertising in Vietnam (the place of the harm). The Swedish woman is upset about the use of her photograph for commercial purposes, which she considers an invasion of her privacy, and she sues the Finnish photographer and the Irish data company for damages and an injunction. Whose law governs?

A rule based on the citizenship of the data creator would mean that those who create data or control it, wherever located, would be subject to the jurisdiction of their sovereign. This rule would track universal personal jurisdiction—the (often unexercised) power of a country to impose rules on its citizens anywhere in the world. Thus, in the example above, Finland's laws would apply because the photographer—the data creator—is Finnish.

However, the Swedish woman has a stronger privacy interest in the photos than the Finnish photographer does. In a globalized world of complex cross-border transactions, the data owner may not be the subject of the data. Thus, a rule based on citizenship of the data subject would mean Sweden's choice-of-law rules apply.

But the Finnish photographer stored the photographs on the Irish company's server. A rule based on the data holder could reinforce geographic aspects of the network. Of course, we might want to differentiate between data holders that claim an ownership interest (say, if the Irish company hired the Finnish photographer and had a contractual agreement for shared ownership of his photographs) and those data holders that claim no such interest.

Finally, consider a rule based on location of the harm. Such a rule would represent a sharp departure from the current system. Rather than focusing on the status of the various parties, the rule would look to the location of the harm. In the above example, this would be Vietnam. None of the four alternatives would provide complete clarity. Some data creators may be dual nationals. Data holders may have corporate headquarters in more than one country. And some events may give rise to harm in more than one country (if the photograph is viewed not only in Vietnam but also in Korea). But these complexities are less easily manipulated than rules based upon data location. A country can anticipate the consequences of litigation by requiring data localization, while individuals, for instance, are unlikely to seek dual citizenship for possible court battles.

Each of the alternatives sketched above has strengths and limitations. The rule based on citizenship of the data creator could provide clarity. Using metadata on the photograph, we can discover its creator. But where the data creator and data subject are different, this rule would undervalue the privacy interests of the data subject.

The rule based on citizenship of the data subject would tie internet choice-of-law rules to a familiar construct: personal jurisdiction. But it might prove difficult to implement. The data subject might not have a clear origin or clear citizenship. Analyzing citizenship retrospectively might prove too difficult.

A rule based on the citizenship of the data holder has the virtue of ease of application. If you are the Irish data holding company, only one rule applies. However, the rule would have the unfortunate consequence of incentivizing data localization—companies would move to areas with the most favorable rather than the most economically efficient rules. Countries would impose lax rules in a race to attract companies.

Finally, a rule based on the location of the harm may seem sensible in theory, and arguably the least susceptible to manipulation. (After all, who knows where the harm will occur?) But different countries can manipulate the definition of the harm; this rule might be implementable only for universally recognized harms (such as murder) and not contested harms (such as the precise definition of "rape").

While none of these rules is perfect, any one would be an improvement over the current disordered process. It is likely that the most practical and fairest rule would apply principles of privacy based on the citizenship of the data subject, but lodge law enforcement authority to seek data in the country of the data holder or in the place where the harm occurred.

Additionally, a transnational agreement—starting in the West—would provide predictability at a time when cross-border disputes are rising. To be effective, governments across the globe need to work concurrently on streamlining the Mutual Legal Assistance Treaty (MLAT) structure. If the case above involved child pornography, Swedish authorities might want information about the Irish data holding company's cybersecurity policy or contracts with the Finnish photographer. If Ireland adopted a cumbersome MLAT process, it could hinder the Swedish police investigation. Ireland would effectively create a data localization safe harbor. An effective network of MLAT treaties must explicitly require a streamlined response as a reciprocal obligation among all signatories.

Chapter Seven

CYBER WARFARE: DETERRENCE AND RESPONSE

A s of the writing of this book, no loss of life has been directly attributed to a cyberattack. However, cyber tools have facilitated military operations.

As described earlier, in 2008, Russian military units crossed into the Ossetia region of the Eurasian country of Georgia, ostensibly to support the independence movement in South Ossetia. The Russian embassy in London described this military operation not as an attack, but rather as a "peace enforcement operation" within Georgia.[1] Curiously, at approximately the same time, a variety of hackers sympathetic to Russia launched waves of cyberattacks. The hackers enlisted a high number of computers (many of which they did not own), or botnets, to attack Georgian websites. Organized on Russian-language sites and blogs, this distributed denial-of-service (DDoS) campaign was intended to overwhelm and incapacitate Georgian government online services, including communications and financial networks. The attacks also defaced websites, gaining access through what is known as a Structured Query Language (SQL) injection.[2] SQL injection takes advantage of a well-known and easy-to-prevent, but nevertheless often overlooked, vulnerability: long strings of characters typed into input fields on webpages can grant unauthorized backdoor access to a webpage's control algorithms. By means of this technique, pictures associating the Georgian president with Adolf Hitler were posted on government websites.[3]

According to some reports, the hackers appeared to be civilian.[4] However, their attacks were clearly timed with the Russian military operations to allow coordination with the physical invasion.[5] The hackers were well prepared. As the attack commenced, they used Russian-language social media forums to recruit other hackers sympathetic to the cause to join the online fight against Georgia. Many of these online forums were created in advance but only activated within 24 hours of the attack.[6] Tools for further attacks were posted, along with instructions on how to join the fight. Target lists, links to malware, and expert advice were provided to aid novice hackers joining the attack.[7]

Initial targets of this malicious online activity included government and news media websites, but the targeting eventually expanded to nearly all important government websites (including those of the presidency, ministries, courts, and parliament), as well as financial and educational institutions. Hackers flooded banks with fraudulent transactions, which prompted international banks to suspend banking operations in Georgia during the conflict. Indeed, the National Bank of Georgia was forced to cut off its internet connection for ten days, halting most of its financial transactions. Cell phone services also failed throughout the country.

This campaign isolated the Georgian government from its citizens and other countries at a crucial time, when it was seeking to resist a Russian invasion. Unlike a DDoS attack against Estonia the year before, the 2008 campaign against Georgia affected the government's ability to defend itself in the physical world. Ultimately, service was restored when internet service providers outside Georgia agreed to host its besieged websites.

As mentioned earlier, a cyberattack on Ukraine that occurred in December 2015 caused physical damage to the power grid. Although attribution in cyberspace is difficult, hackers with a connection to Russia were believed to be the culprits. The attack was performed by serious actors with the knowledge, skills, and operational planning necessary to deploy multiple malware tools. Custom-made malicious software tools, along with readily available malware, were used to gain access to and disrupt power at three different companies. The hackers understood details about the control systems and targeted the deletion of specific activity logs.[8] Some malware found in the substation cyberattack is readily available and similar to that found in other exploits by Russian activists, though the activities of the intruders revealed that they had performed deep reconnaissance to develop knowledge of the targeted systems and create reasonably sophisticated capabilities to attack. In this case, again, the effect was not merely to knock a computer network offline or to block its use, but to damage or destroy physical assets in order to slow the restoration of electricity. The episode shows how malicious cyber activity has evolved beyond mere nuisance or theft of data to the destruction of physical assets as part of a geopolitical struggle. Some speculate that the Russia cyberattack on Ukraine sought to intimidate the country's parliament and dissuade it from nationalizing privately owned power companies in the country.[9]

Earlier, I discussed the 2012 attack that took place against oil giant Saudi Aramco. That attack employed the Shamoon virus and affected more than 30,000 computers. It destroyed significant informational infrastructure and caused delays in petroleum delivery and distribution. Just two weeks after the Saudi Aramco attacks, the Qatari natural gas producer RasGas was attacked with a similar virus. The attack shut down local email servers but did not appear to affect gas production. Both Iran and Hezbollah are suspected of involvement in the attacks on Saudi Aramco and RasGas.[10] If true, this would mean Iran has acquired potent capabilities after suffering attacks on its own infrastructure in 2010.[11]

Then, the Stuxnet worm caused physical damage to Iranian centrifuges used for enriching uranium for nuclear purposes. No party has yet claimed credit for the attack, though David Sanger, an investigative journalist, has attributed it to both Israel and the United States.[12] Whoever created Stuxnet hid it deep within the control system of the centrifuges. After clandestine installment on the machines, the worm sat idle, monitoring the plant's "normal operation." At the appropriate time, it falsely "played back" the

normal operation to the control systems while simultaneously forcing the centrifuges to spin out of control. This
caused catastrophic physical damage. Seeing normal readings on their control systems, the centrifuge operators were
initially clueless about the attack and later became distrustful
of their own instruments.[13]

Cyberattacks that can cause physical destruction are
no longer science fiction. Theft of data, fraudulent exploitation of the internet for financial gain, theft of intellectual
property, and even nation-state espionage are the types
of activities that have traditionally been addressed by law
enforcement or, in the case of espionage, diplomacy. But
using cyberattacks to damage or destroy data or physical
operations could be deemed an act of war, warranting a
military response.

The Definition of "Warfare"
and the Problem of Attribution

Whether a destructive act is regarded as criminal activity,
warfare, or a murky hybrid generally depends on a variety
of factors. These include (1) how clearly the act is attribut-
able to a government; (2) whether the act is undertaken by
private actors that are effectively controlled by a government; (3) the intent of the perpetrator; and (4) the effects
of the attack.

In cyberspace, traditional legal and policy distinctions
between crime and warfare start to break down. Several
conceptual legal problems emerge. For one, the difference
between criminal destruction and warfare could be merely a

matter of degree of effect. Perhaps the *purpose* of a destructive attack is relevant. And must the malicious actor be a nation-state to trigger war footing, or can nonstate groups, such as sympathetic activists, mount an act of war? In 2001, for example, we invaded Afghanistan, holding the country accountable for Osama bin Laden's September 11, 2001, attack. It is also unclear under international law if the disruption or destruction of internet access or availability counts as a "use of force" or an "armed attack."

Resolving these issues would determine whether a country should respond to cyberattacks with law enforcement, counterintelligence, or the military; whether a besieged country can use force in self-defense under international law and call upon allies under collective defense treaties; and to what extent the laws of war apply in limiting armed conflict.

The boundless geography of cyberspace makes the relationship between private actors and nation-states particularly challenging. In physical conflict, combatants are present on or proximate to the battlefield. In cyber conflict, attacks can be launched from a desktop thousands of miles away, passing through multiple pathways and routers. The attackers are not visible and do not wear uniforms. They are often not subject to a military command-and-control structure. As we have seen in the cases of Russian attacks on Georgia and Ukraine, a nation-state may sponsor and encourage private hackers by ignoring or failing to investigate activities when they further that nation's political or military interests. This sort of hybrid warfare has been a recent feature of physical conflict (as witnessed in the 2014 invasion of Crimea), but it is even more prevalent in the cyber domain. It raises difficult questions about whether a government can be held accountable if it is deemed to be controlling private actors carrying out cyberattacks.

Finally, a special challenge is posed by the use of cyber tools to engage in information operations (or information warfare). These tactics are designed to confuse the population of an adversary or undermine its confidence. Embarrassing information might be leaked or even phony documents distributed. During the so-called Maidan revolution, in which the pro-Russian president of Ukraine was ousted, hackers sympathetic to Russia released what was purported to be a recorded conversation of two U.S. officials encouraging the uprising. More recently, the U.S. Department of Homeland Security and the director of National Intelligence have stated that the Russian government directed cyber intrusions at U.S. political parties and organizations, leading to the selective release of documents designed to embarrass certain U.S. political figures. In 2016, the major U.S. intelligence agencies publicized a definitive finding that Russian government-sponsored hackers were behind the theft and dissemination of emails from the Democratic National Committee. Former DHS secretary Jeh Johnson testified before the U.S. Congress in June 2017 that "in 2016 the Russian government, at the direction of Vladimir Putin himself, orchestrated cyber-attacks on our nation for the purpose of influencing our election—plain and simple."[14]

Other DHS officials noted that state and local voter databases were also penetrated by Russian hackers, although there is no evidence votes were altered or deleted. A Russian agent penetrated the State of Illinois voter registration database and sought unsuccessfully to download files on 15 million voters. In all, more than 20 local election databases were penetrated by Russian hacking, with a number showing efforts to affect voter-roll information. These penetrations highlight the real risk of an effort to tamper with the electoral process in the United States by deleting or altering voter registrations, or conveying misleading information about how and where to vote.[15]

Do efforts to manipulate electoral processes or actually physically interfere with voting cross the line into acts of war? While the former smacks of propaganda, which does not normally trigger actual belligerence, a physical disruption of voting approaches an attack on critical infrastructure.

Deterring and Responding to Cyber Warfare

Given the novelty of cyber conflict and the still-evolving international norms applicable to cyber warfare,[16] there has yet to be articulated a clear doctrine about how to effectively deter or respond to a cyberattack, even if it causes serious physical effects. Some of the difficulty arises from uncertainty over when those effects cross the line into what would be clearly regarded as armed aggression. But there is also not yet a fully mature understanding about how to calibrate strategy for a deterrence policy that is neither so weak as to invite attack nor, on the other hand, prone to recklessly escalate minor incidents. Cyberwar deterrence doctrine currently resembles the early days of nuclear deterrence strategy, but the issue is far more complex: early nuclear deterrence involved only two main nuclear powers, whereas the power to engage in cyber warfare is widely distributed around the globe.

To be sure, ambiguity can be helpful in deterring undesirable cyber operations. Understandably, the U.S. government has not drawn crystal-clear lines about what counts as an act of war in cyberspace. The U.S. Department of Defense *Law of War Manual* acknowledges that the application of the law of war to cyberspace "is not well-settled" and that the law is "likely to continue to develop."[17] The manual lists some examples of cyber operations that the U.S. government would be likely to consider illegal uses of force under international law and that would thus trigger the right to use force in self-defense.[18] They include cyber operations that "trigger a nuclear plant meltdown; . . . open a dam above a populated area, causing destruction; . . . disable air traffic control services, resulting in airplane crashes; . . . [or] cripple a military's logistics systems, and thus its ability to conduct and sustain military operations ."[19] While the examples involve "cyber activities that proximately result in death, injury, or significant destruction,"[20] the manual does not clarify what, if any, kinds of lesser cyber-produced effects might trigger the use of force in self-defense. After all, not every cyber activity has a direct parallel with physical uses of force.

At his nomination hearing before the Senate Armed Services Committee in 2015, Secretary of Defense Ash Carter was asked what he believed would constitute an act of war in cyberspace. In response, he focused on the effects of a cyber operation:

> I believe that what is termed an act of war should follow the same practice as in other domains, because it is the seriousness, not the means, of an attack that matters most.
>
> Whether a particular attack is considered an "act of war," in or out of cyberspace, requires a determination on a case-by-case and fact-specific basis. Malicious cyber activities could result in death, injury or significant destruction, and any such activities would be regarded with the utmost concern and could well be considered "acts of war." An attack does not need to be deemed an "act of war" to require a response.[21]

One gray area in particular warrants consideration: How do we treat information operations—propaganda—over the internet that are a feature of what is sometimes called "hybrid warfare"? When a nation-state undertakes so-called information operations, they may include factual misinformation designed to confuse other national publics and sap cohesiveness and the will to fight; trolling and online intimidation aimed at silencing critics; theft and publication of sensitive documents designed to be politically or personally embarrassing to adversaries (called "doxing"); and even interference in and disruption of governmental and financial functions, as was seen for example in the 2007 denial-of-service attacks against Estonian government and banking networks.

Such information operations are not destructive in the way that could be readily characterized as warfare. Yet they are not mere crime; for geopolitical purposes, they are efforts to strategically undermine another nation's will to fight. A response in kind would be surely warranted, but few would argue that the response should escalate to violence or physical combat. A range of responses should be formulated, including promotion of counternarratives, economic sanctions, and even blocking or disabling online platforms that launch these information operations.

Deterrence Is More Difficult Because of the Challenge of Attribution

In addition to determining what activities in cyberspace rise to the level of acts of war, identifying the culprits is also a challenge. A typical feature of cyberattacks is for hackers to move malicious software through multiple servers to mask the originating source of an attack. The ease with which malicious actors can obscure their presence online has led many commentators to describe what is known as the "problem of attribution" in cyberspace. In the physical world, it is usually possible to identify the source of a military attack of significant size by monitoring the launching point. To be sure, the ability to attribute in the physical world is not perfect. Activities in Ukraine and Crimea in 2015 showed how even conventional military activities could be denied, and ambiguity could create confusion in the middle of a crisis. Even as the Russian role became clearer, the ability to determine which leaders authorized what activities, and to what end, remained elusive.

In the aggregate, though, the ability to precisely attribute malicious behavior is more difficult in cyberspace, where even a massive destructive payload can be launched from a thumb drive. An attack can be physically launched from almost anywhere, and the origin of an attack can be obfuscated by sending it through remotely controlled machines. Just as in a real-life murder scene, investigators search for evidence and examine all trails leading back to the perpetrators. Sleuths in physical attacks seek to prove that an act was carried out by an accused individual present at the location with motive and opportunity. In cyber investigations, the perpetrator is almost never physically present at the location of the attack. Investigators must follow the behavior of the malware and attempt to reverse-engineer it to understand intent. Among the clues are the languages used, or comments left behind in the code. Detectives may focus on what the malware code was trying to do, what it was *not* doing, and if it was similar to other malware. Military scholar Thomas Rid and cyber security expert Ben Buchanan describe attribution as a nuanced, artistic process in which

> there is no one recipe for correct attribution, no one methodology or flow-chart or check-list. Finding the right clues requires a disciplined focus on a set of detailed questions—but also the intuition of technically experienced operators. . . . On an operational level, *attribution is a nuanced process, not a simple problem.*

That process of attribution is not binary, but measured in uneven degrees, it is not black-and-white, yes-or-no, but appears in shades. As a result, it is also a team sport—successful attribution requires more skills and resources than any single mind can offer.[22]

Even if the attack can be tracked all the way back to the individual machine used to launch it, identifying the person behind the screen can be difficult. According to political scientists P. W. Singer and Allan Friedman, "Establishing attribution is not the same as establishing complicity. It is sometimes possible to track an actor's efforts to a certain geographic locale, but it is more difficult to establish any formal government role, whether as perpetrator or sanctioner of the operation."[23] The attack may have been intentional or merely an accident. Or the ostensible attackers may have been manipulated by someone else. Even more problematic is making a determination whether the malicious act was sanctioned by a nation-state or performed by a lone actor.

Foggy attribution reduces our ability to deter. If the person or group responsible can't be identified, then we have trouble discouraging malicious behavior. The problem is complicated because cyberattacks can be routed through infrastructure in neutral third countries, further disguising a cyber aggressor's identity. Even if a malicious actor can be identified, if it is a nonstate actor, there may be no physical assets to sanction. Because individuals and nation-states are able to obfuscate attribution in cyberspace, threats to punish tend to have lower credibility. Former deputy secretary of defense William J. Lynn III thus wrote, "Deterrence will necessarily be based more on denying any benefit to attackers than on imposing costs through retaliation."[24]

There are signs, however, that the problem of attribution in cyberspace may be changing. Governments are not as new to this problem as they were a decade ago. In a speech given from the retired aircraft carrier USS *Intrepid* stationed in New York, then–secretary of defense Leon Panetta emphasized the government's strides in identifying the source of cyberattacks:

> Our cyber adversaries will be far less likely to hit us if they know that we will be able to link to the attack or that their effort will fail against our strong defenses. The department has made significant advances in solving a problem that makes deterring cyber adversaries more complex: the difficulty of identifying the origins of that attack. . . . Over the last two years, DoD has made significant investments in forensics to address this problem of attribution and we're seeing the returns on that investment. Potential aggressors should be aware that the United States has the capacity to locate them and to hold them accountable for their actions that may try to harm America.[25]

Even if the threshold of certainty of attribution that would justify a military retaliatory response is viewed as relatively high, less dramatic responses to cyberattacks might still have a deterrent effect. These include economic sanctions, criminal charges, and other forms of "naming and shaming." For example, after the United States charged members of the People's Liberation Army with commercial cyber espionage in 2013, the Chinese government eventually agreed to reduce commercial cyber hacking. In 2014, the Obama administration publicly accused North Korea of hacking into Sony Pictures, where it destroyed the Hollywood studio's physical computer systems and stole sensitive data, including screenplays for unreleased movies.[26]

Even more dramatically, in 2016 the U.S. intelligence community formally called out Russian intelligence agencies for hacking into the Democratic National Committee database, and the Department of Justice indicted two Russian intelligence agents for hacking 500 million user accounts on Yahoo.

To be sure, there are costs to even making official accusations against another nation, including antagonizing the alleged perpetrator, setting a precedent that increases pressure to identify future malicious actors, and revealing sensitive sources and methods that the government typically wants to keep secret in order to continue gathering valuable intelligence.

An alternative way of embarrassing or frustrating a nation-state hacker is to rely on private sector cybersecurity research firms to publicize attribution by releasing open-source articles that link an intrusion to a likely perpetrator. The court of public opinion does not require evidence "beyond a reasonable doubt." Even if these research firms don't have conclusive proof of precisely who was responsible, exposure of information about the attackers enables others to investigate further and highlights a threat avenue that puts other potential victims on alert. Private security companies that expose nation-state hacking do not need to struggle with the broader geopolitical considerations that come when one government formally accuses another of cyber aggression.

By means of encouraging private firms to investigate and attribute nation-state hacking, the general public's awareness can be advanced. That happened in 2013, when the *New York Times* hired the Mandiant computer security company to investigate penetrations into its networks. Mandiant helped track the perpetrators to a specific set of internet addresses assigned to the Shanghai premises of a Chinese military unit. Using social media and other clues, the newspaper was able to identify two individual hackers.[27] As noted earlier, the U.S. Justice Department subsequently indicted five members of the People's Liberation Army on charges of cyber espionage. By publicly reporting these conclusions, the *Times* educated the public about Chinese theft of American companies' trade secrets, and may well have embarrassed China into modifying its behavior.[28]

We should also broaden the definition of what constitutes state responsibility for cyberattacks and what constitutes an act of war. As discussed, the relationship between private hackers and government authorities is often deliberately shrouded in obscurity to generate official deniability. If a state can be held accountable for a destructive attack only with clear proof of official sponsorship, it will often be difficult—especially within the constraints of operational secrecy—to demonstrate actual state responsibility. Under such a narrow definition of state responsibility, deterrence would be weakened because it would be more difficult to trigger mutual self-defense treaties, such as NATO Article 5, or the right of self-defense under the U.N. Charter.

To be sure, a state responding to a cyberattack might justify its attribution of the perpetrator by referring to secret evidence or circumstantial evidence. And with a serious act of cyber aggression, the responding state might simply act on its own conclusion about attribution. But as a comparison with the Iraq War suggests, making a case for a response under international law and building international support often lead to more sustainable outcomes, both globally and domestically.

The solution is to take a broad view of state responsibility; under this rule, if a country knowingly tolerates attacks launched from its territory, that suffices to attribute responsibility for these acts. If the subject of an attack traces the launch to a computer server in State X, it is appropriate to demand that State X stop the attack and punish the attackers, or be held accountable as a sponsor. The failure of State X to shut down the aggression might justify a direct response against the attackers as well as punitive retaliation against the nation that encourages or ignores attacks. Under this broad view of deterrence, the presumption of attribution focuses on the state from which the cyberattack is launched, creating incentives for that state to police the behavior of hackers within its borders.

Active Defense and the Problem of Privateers

Some argue that where the "host" government can't or won't stop cyberattacks (whether destructive or merely larcenous), then the victim should have the right to respond—what is sometimes called "active defense." The U.S. military and intelligence agencies already use active defense systems, described as "part sensor, part sentry, part sharpshooter," to automatically counter cyber intrusions in real time.[29] The question arises as to whether the private sector should be allowed to engage in active defense, too.

Active defense raises the flip side of the earlier question about the extent of state responsibility for private hackers—namely, whether private parties who are victims of cyberattacks should be able to retaliate. But what starts as defense against criminal destruction could escalate into warfare, for which the state itself would then be accountable. Should the government have the exclusive right to trigger such escalating conduct?[30]

The definition of active defense as applied to cyberspace is contested, but at its core it involves maneuverability and adaptability to counter persistent and dangerous threats.[31] An active defender will "monitor for, respond to, and learn from adversaries."[32] There is a spectrum of acts that can be characterized as active defense. The most minimal—and probably unobjectionable—are passive, analytical actions, such as creating a "honeypot" of apparently attractive targets that lure and trap malware for forensic analysis.

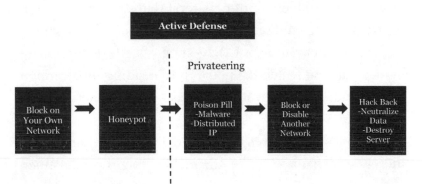

At the other end of the spectrum is "hacking back," which involves pursuing the attacker and responding by either neutralizing the stolen data or incapacitating the server from which the attack was launched. An October 2016 study by a task force at the Center for Cyber and Homeland Security (which I cochaired) observed that between these two poles there is a range of active defensive steps.[33]

There are at least two objections to hacking back—one legal, the other practical. Legally, we do not normally permit private victims to engage in self-help to retaliate or neutralize their attacker. (This is to be distinguished from self-defense, which prevents an attack rather than retaliates against one.) Practically, there is no assurance that a private party can surgically limit a response; hacking back could fail to be effective (say, in wiping stolen data) and it could also escalate the problem. Nor can a private party be sure of the true identity of the perpetrator. Indeed, as discussed above, the government is not always able to attribute; for example, in 1999, the Pentagon was able to trace exfiltration of data from the U.S. Air Force—maps of military installations and hardware designs—to a computer in Russia but failed to attribute any political actor or clear motive.[34] Hacking back raises considerable risk of collateral damage, or escalation to nation-state conflict. Hacking back also risks making a private conflict public: a U.S. company's effort to retaliate by neutralizing stolen data currently residing on a foreign server could be perceived abroad as hacking sanctioned by the U.S. government.

Even more aggressive would be private action not merely to defend but to retaliate. This might be explained as future deterrence, although it is hard to discern a principled justification for this policy.

There are two middle positions that warrant debate, and even legislation. One is to embed the honeypot with malware, so an attack on the target and theft of information have the effect of exfiltrating malware back to the attacker's own network. This has the benefit of hoisting the attacker with his own petard, since it is his own theft that exposes his network to damage. But this does not entirely eliminate the risk of collateral damage, as a shrewd attacker may lodge stolen data in a proxy server owned by innocent parties.

A more modest position is to embed the honeypot not with malware but with false or marked information. In the former case, one who steals intellectual property actually has his effort misdirected, since what he seeks to exploit may be nonfunctional. It is worth noting, however, that if a malicious actor has fully penetrated a corporation's network, it will often be able to uncover the corporation's attempt to plant false or marked information. Perhaps more usefully, secretly tagging stolen intellectual property might allow the owner to later lodge a claim against anyone seeking to benefit from the data theft.

What role should the government play in licensing private response? The U.S. Constitution provides that "Congress shall have Power . . . To declare War, grant Letters of Marque and Reprisal, and make Rules concerning Captures on Land and Water."[35] Letters of marque were formal authorizations for privateers to capture enemy ships. In early U.S. history, this practice allowed the government to augment its fleet at low cost and regulate private action on the high seas; private ship captains could get a cut of the profits from capturing and plundering enemy vessels.[36] During the undeclared war with France from 1798 to 1800, for instance, Congress passed statutes providing rewards for the recapture of American vessels.[37] In a case from that time, Supreme Court opinions framed international hostilities in terms of "perfect war" and "imperfect war."[38] If a "perfect," or declared, war triggered specific international law rules of belligerency and neutrality, an "imperfect," or undeclared, war might only have involved hostilities among certain parties, such as those authorized by letters of marque.[39]

Using the analogy to letters of marque and reprisal, the government could approve certain private acts in cyberspace, such as retaliation.[40] Just as American and French vessels fought without triggering a formal, all-out war, the United States could fight its enemies in cyberspace by licensing private actors. As a matter of domestic law, the Constitution could be interpreted such that letters of marque would allow Congress to authorize cyber privateers. As a matter of international law, the Paris Declaration of Maritime Law of 1856 purported to abolish privateering;[41] however, the United States did not ratify the declaration, so it is not binding on U.S. actions. Notwithstanding the Paris Declaration, states have continued to use letters of marque to counter piracy and authorize self-defense in some cases,[42] although this practice has not fully developed into customary international law (that is, consistent state practice followed out of a sense of legal obligation).[43] Although ambiguous, international law could arguably permit self-defense against cyber pirates.

Granting letters of marque could bolster U.S. resources devoted to protecting U.S. information against theft and sabotage. As Oxford University cyber scholar Florian Egloff has observed, "the cultivation and utilisation of private talent for economic wealth transfer is the modern version of privateering."[44] Apple, Facebook, Google, Microsoft, Verizon—these multinational information technology companies are driven by profits, but they also have interests substantially aligned with those of the United States: free exchange of information, economic integration, technological development, and protection of private property, including trade secrets. Authorizing such actors to actively defend their own networks could help stem the theft of intellectual property and other sensitive data.[45]

But letters of marque would have costs. The government would have difficulty controlling private responses. Unintended consequences could escalate conflicts. Private actors with the resources to conduct hack-backs would include multinational corporations that might hesitate to run afoul of foreign laws prohibiting hack-backs.[46] Moreover, letters of marque would prevent the United States from asserting plausible deniability, and could alert foreign adversaries to at least some U.S. capabilities. Licensing private actors could undermine our ability to condemn others doing so. It could put pressure on the United States to halt cyber operations from actors whose actions align with U.S. interests.

Protecting the U.S. civilian cyber infrastructure is critical to preserving the vitality of our economy and national defense, and the U.S. Department of Homeland Security has a mammoth task in protecting .gov and .com addresses. To bolster its capacity to defend and deter cyberattacks, the government should train and license "privateers" for certain specific operations, such as to create honeypots with tagged information or to assist in deterring attacks against U.S. companies and infrastructure. To minimize unintended consequences, however, the government should absolutely prohibit private retaliation and restrict cyber defensive activities to those under active supervision by the government authorities.

How Do U.S. Legal Authorities Change in a Borderless Cyber Battlefield?

The laws of war are often pegged to the existence of a battlefield. But cyberattacks or retaliations are executed over the same networks that carry civilian communications traffic. In response to a cyberattack, is it justifiable then to treat a network infrastructure as fair game? As modern geopolitical conflict increasingly looks to economic power as a weapon (e.g., financial sanctions), platforms that host economic activity become part of the battlefield.

Cyber warfare is executed in a borderless surface area, and attacks on U.S. infrastructure could be launched by an enemy with a thumb drive in a cybercafé in Austin, Texas. For the purposes of U.S. defense and security agencies, it no longer makes sense to pretend there is a clear distinction between law enforcement and military action. Traditionally, our American legal structure is premised on the view that war involves a delineated battlefield, almost always overseas. Under U.S. law such as *posse comitatus*, therefore, there is a clear line drawn between domestic law enforcement, which is off-limits to the military; and military combat, on which the armed forces take the lead. But the foreign and domestic distinction that underpins much of the structure of government authority under Titles 10 (armed forces), 18 (criminal law), and 50 (intelligence) is not applicable in an environment in which the attack may be launched from imputed servers not only around the globe but also within the United States. It is unclear how *posse comitatus* applies when a foreign enemy attack is directed from a server sitting in a coffee shop in the United States. The geography of the server no longer matters. When a cyberattack rises to the level of war, our response must blend military and law enforcement authorities.

Similar reformulation of our legal architecture is necessary in intelligence collection. The restrictions in collecting involving U.S. persons that normally govern intelligence collection should not fully apply when a foreign government hijacks an American's computer to mount an attack. And these issues must be adjudicated at network speed. Perhaps a judicial warrant should not be required in the exigent case where government needs to access the American-based server that is in the process of degrading critical infrastructure. This would be similar to the public safety exception to warrant requirements when emergency action is needed to prevent imminent physical peril. Many of the distinctions that lie at the heart of our laws governing the authorities of the intelligence community do not fit a world of cyber conflict and cyber threats that are heedless of the distinction between domestic and foreign.

Putting aside issues of how U.S. law operates, armed conflict in the domain of cyberspace poses challenging questions relating to the application of the international law of armed conflict. For example, a cardinal principle of that law is that innocent civilians may not be the object of attacks, and reasonable steps must be taken to avoid incidental injuries to civilians that are the by-product of a permissible attack on military forces. But in cyberspace, it may be ambiguous when a civilian has crossed the line into engaging in cyber combat. Protecting and maintaining a computer network that performs military functions could constitute direct participation in an attack against an enemy. So, too, could designing cyber tools for other uses that can be transformed into offensive hacking tools to damage an enemy command-and-control system.[47]

Only military "objects" can be lawfully targeted, and such an object is generally defined as "something 'visible and tangible.'" But it's unclear whether data is an "object." While computer infrastructure is tangible, the data that flows across or rests within networks or "smart" devices is not. On the other hand, if the data is destroyed, the usefulness of the physical "smart" device is as well. That has given rise to debate about whether data can be a legitimate military target. Conversely, if data is not an "object," data that is civilian in nature might be unprotected under a literal interpretation of existing law.[48]

In the physical world, there are some objects that can be dual use—helpful to sustaining military action but also essential for purely civilian purposes. An example would be a seaport used to berth naval vessels. Under accepted principles of law, one can target the seaport as a military object, taking reasonable care to avoid damaging elements of the port that serve civilian functions only. But in cyberspace, infrastructure used for military purposes may well be the same used for purely civilian purposes. The digital packets flowing over the infrastructure may simultaneously include military and civilian data elements. Logically, one might argue that the entire internet, or a substantial portion, is a military object. The line between a permissible and an impermissible target gets very blurry.

The internet's geographically indeterminate quality and functional interchangeability mean that traditional laws and rules governing military and intelligence authorities and armed conflict do not fit comfortably. While the values of limiting military authorities in a democracy, and protecting civilians in wartime, remain as vital as ever, their application in the new landscape of Data 3.0 requires greater flexibility in how and where the military is allowed to execute its missions.

MEETING THE CHALLENGE OF DATA 3.0: RECOMMENDATIONS FOR LAW AND POLICY

In our world of big data, we want to give the government the appropriate legal authority to provide security while maintaining a sufficient scope of privacy and autonomy necessary for our human dignity. Citizens seek to enjoy the convenience and efficiency of modern commercial data-driven technology without putting their security and freedom at risk.

With its ability to generate and review huge amounts of data, today's technology numbs society, creating social acceptance for our loss of privacy. Given the ease with which emails, telephone metadata, and other previously private forms of information are captured by others, Americans have been surrendering control over electronic privacy. Today's legal framework attempts to protect the right to privacy under a technology assumption that is decades old. We have come to accept the fact that our emails may be read, and we have become accustomed to our data being collected and used by others.

If privacy means the ability to hide or shield our actions and thoughts from prying eyes, that privacy ship has sailed. The volume of data we generate and the analytic power that can be applied against our data mean that few of us can remain opaque. I argue that the focus of our concern should shift to protecting our autonomy. We should maintain a reasonable degree of ownership of and control over the data that we generate or that relates to us.

In past times, evolving enhancements in the power of the government to conduct surveillance on its own citizens have been checked by recalibrating the scope of our individual liberties. As technology progresses, the balance should shift appropriately.

Recall that under *Olmstead v. United States*, the courts weighed an individual's privacy rights against the government's need to listen in on conversations. In his dissent, Justice Brandeis argued that "there is, in essence, no difference between the sealed letter and the private telephone message."[1] When weighing unfettered wiretapping access for the government against individual privacy rights, Justice Brandeis provided a thoughtful dissent, arguing that it is the information in a private letter or telephone message that must be protected as private, not merely the physical integrity of the mode of communication.

But the lesson of history is not only that rules adapt to protect individual autonomy by restraining government power as new invasive technologies develop. Laws also change to encourage the government to more actively wield its authority to protect against undue concentration of power in unaccountable private hands. That occurred during the administration of President Teddy Roosevelt, which marshaled federal antitrust laws to break up highly concentrated wealth and power in private enterprises. Similarly, anti-wiretapping laws were extended to private corporations and citizens to protect our privacy.

So, as we have seen, privacy and freedom must mean more than freedom from government surveillance. We also need protection from the danger of private surveillance that may become ubiquitous and even coercive. Here, too, however, today's legal and social framework protecting our privacy from corporations is no longer sufficient. Without comprehending the extent of our consent, we freely give away our data to private companies in consent forms that are pages long, with a simple checkmark or click.

To be sure, we could say no to consent forms that are too long, too complicated, or without limits. But when the service that seeks our consent is a monopoly, and we have no choice but to consent as a condition of obtaining a necessary service, then government antitrust authorities should place limits on the scope of consent that is demanded. Moreover, corporations to which we have never given consent sometimes use data we generate without explicit legal permission simply because it is unclear who really "owns" the digital information.

When technology has dramatically expanded the ability to monitor activities in a previously unrealizable way, we need a new set of laws. We saw how the founders designed the Constitution to protect privacy through private property, and how the law evolved in response to the telegraph and telephone to also protect conversations. Today, technology has dramatically expanded the ability of not just governments but also corporations and individuals to collect, store, and analyze digital data. It is once again time for Congress and the courts to recalibrate law and policy.

Inevitably, this will require trade-offs between different values: privacy, autonomy, security, and the individual versus the collective interest. Trying to fit new technology into old vessels breaks or distorts the vessels. We must create new vessels, but this project must be informed by what we are trying to protect.

I opened this book with a few scenarios. Brian and Kate were caring parents who wished to give their daughter the best, but who unwittingly "consented" to an invasion of privacy by getting her a Talkie Terry doll from Omnicorp. Well-meaning privacy-law professor Carl faced higher insurance rates because of his digital exhaust. And remember James, who lived a perfectly programmed life under the supervision and control of the "organization." We must prevent the worst features of these scenarios from becoming our reality.

Five Specific Frameworks for New Laws and Rules Can Block These Scenarios

First, to protect us against attacks on our physical security and cybersecurity by bad actors while simultaneously preventing the government from overreaching to threaten our autonomy, we must recognize that Data 3.0 requires both a loosening of what information can be collected by government and at the same time a tightening of the standards under which that information can be inspected, analyzed, and used. We should grant the government relatively broad authority to access and collect data. The government cannot effectively disrupt criminal enterprises or foil terrorist plots without following a digital data trail that may appear significant only with the passage of time. The trail goes cold if the government does not have initial access and collection capability so that the relationships in the data can be analyzed in context. Note, however, that I am not advocating that private companies build vulnerabilities, like decryption backdoors, into their systems to assist the government. The government should use its own resources; this burden remains on the government.

But even as restrictions on access and collection are loosened, restraints on government inspection (human or robot), analysis, dissemination, and use of that data should be tightened to strengthen civil liberties protections against its abuse. In the interest of individual autonomy, this balances the need to preserve useful information with the need to control human access—and possible misuse—of that information.

Second, consider the spectrum of active defense when our enterprises or homes are attacked by cyber criminals, terrorists, or adversary nation-states. I suggest that licensing private actors to defend their networks could help the United States stem the theft of intellectual property—the greatest heist in history. But to mitigate the risks of unintended consequences and uncontrolled escalation of conflict, the government must restrict these licenses to specific activities and set clear rules of the road. In particular, no private party should be allowed to retaliate against or invade another network—even if it is the source of a hacking attack—except under the direction and control of an appropriate law enforcement or judicial authority.

Third, to avoid fragmentation of the internet, and the consequent huge global economic cost, Congress should work with other countries to develop uniformity in both the legal process for obtaining data and the substantive laws governing that data. This will require the creation of enforceable treaties or international agreements that focus on protecting the rights of the data subject, since the focus of personal autonomy is reasonable control over one's own data. The objective of this developing international law regime should be to avoid inconsistencies that lead to individual national laws that mandate data localization and thereby compromise the global architecture and freedom of movement of internet data.

Fourth, the law must evolve to control the use private parties can make of individual data. In a world in which people inevitably give off digital exhaust and often cannot provide meaningful consent to the use of their data by apps or third parties, the law should shift the default to better protect privacy and autonomy. As some European regulators are currently insisting, this means that enterprises seeking to use data for purposes other than improving the particular service engaged by the user—for example, reselling to third-party marketers—should be required to obtain that user's affirmative or "opt in" consent. Even more explicit consent from the data subject should be mandated when a data aggregator or platform seeks to resell or repurpose an individual's data that was obtained from the third parties that initially collected that subject's data without consent. For those aggregators or platforms whose market position makes them effective monopolists, consent may be deemed insufficient; regulators may need to impose limits on the data uses a monopolist may engage in, and might even require that a fee be paid by the company to the subject for certain uses.

Most important, the law must limit the ability of corporations to coerce individuals into consenting to broad surrender of control over their data. Thus, the ability of employers or insurance providers to insist on virtually limitless access to individual data as a condition of employment or affordable premiums should be tailored to apply only to information reasonably related to employment or insurability. And data collected for these reasons should be barred from resale or use for unrelated purposes.

Indeed, noting that nongovernmental organizations have developed transparency indices for how well tech companies respond to government requests for their users' data, we should develop transparent accounts or regulations for how private companies are using and, especially, sharing individual users' data.[2]

Fifth, the law must incentivize private parties to collaborate with the government in protecting against shared vulnerabilities. The vast majority of IT infrastructure is in private hands, but the internet makes it interdependent. Without government expertise and even regulation, coupled with private sector ingenuity and commitment, the internet infrastructure will continue to fall prey to its weakest link. As part of this effort, the law should encourage and protect information sharing directly and in real time among private and public entities on both industry-focused and regional bases.

We Citizens Need to Own Our Internet

If there is an overarching lesson to be drawn from the technology revolution that is Data 3.0, it is that our day-to-day lives are described and even defined by data. We generate data, which tracks our behavior, preferences, location, and even intentions. Data is used to incentive us, deter us, and even coerce us. If others, be they government or private actors, manage our data, they effectively control much of what we do.

The internet was intended as a force to empower individuals, to forge global connectivity, and even to promote freedom. Although some believe that the internet can be a law-free, almost anarchic zone, this book has demonstrated that, without thoughtful rules, the internet can be a tool to constrain individual autonomy, to bully, and to manipulate.

One way to look at the sea of data in which we currently swim is as a global public good. Such a public good has value only if there are rules that prohibit overreaching interference and disruption. We must therefore develop rules to prevent powerful institutions and bad actors from using internet data to damage, rather than enhance, our autonomy.

ACKNOWLEDGMENTS

This book was born from years of working with intelligence, security, and law enforcement issues that exposed me to the valuable uses—and abuses—of our rapidly expanding data universe. A number of the ideas that form the core of this work were aired in op-eds, articles, speeches, and less formal discussions.

The idea of bringing this together in a book was encouraged and facilitated by Professor Graham Allison, a prolific scholar, the former dean of the Harvard University Kennedy School's Belfer Center, and a friend. Graham encouraged me to commit to producing a volume, generously offered me the intellectual support of members of the Belfer Center, and introduced me to his literary agent.

Through Graham, I had the opportunity to work with two brilliant scholars: Scott McEntire, a military veteran and Belfer scholar; and Dan Severson, a Harvard Law student and now lawyer. Scott and Dan helped shape the book, did extensive research, drafted passages, and devoted enormous effort to this enterprise. Other experts at the Belfer Center who devoted time and effort to discussing my ideas and furnishing useful comments were Michael Sulmeyer, Bruce Schneier, Joseph Nye, and Anne Boustead, as well as a number of students who asked questions and made suggestions at various open forums organized by Graham.

At my consulting firm, the Chertoff Group, I had the invaluable assistance of a number of colleagues who have worked with me over the years on policy issues and who have teamed up with me in producing articles and speeches, which form much of the intellectual underpinnings of this book. Paul Rosenzweig has been my coauthor on a number of pieces. Katy Montgomery has prompted my thinking on many of the areas in this volume, and has been a crack editor. Alan Wehler has been a fount of knowledge and an inveterate researcher, and took on the task of reviewing my draft text, checking sourcing, and making important suggestions. Meggie Trusty, my executive assistant, cheerfully took on the task of assembling the final product, coordinating edits, and managing logistics. The book could not have been finished without them.

I gained other valuable insights through my work on the Global Commission on Internet Governance, ably chaired by Carl Bildt and Gordon Smith; with Fen Hampson of the Centre for International Governance Innovation; and with Patricia Lewis of Chatham House.

My editors George Gibson and Dana Isaacson, and agent Michael Carlisle, skillfully steered me through the process of shaping a manuscript into a book, and turning it into a published work. Their advice was invaluable.

Countless others have contributed intellectual capital to my work, including clients, law firm colleagues, and friends. Of course, the responsibility for all errors of fact or analysis rests entirely with me.

This book certainly could not have been started, let alone finished, without the support and advice of my wife, Meryl; daughter, Emily; and son, Philip. Throughout, they offered helpful suggestions and comments, and inspired, encouraged, and sustained me.

NOTES

Introduction: Big Data Is Watching You

1. Andrea Thomas, "Germany Issues Kill Order for a Domestic Spy—Cayla the Toy Doll," *Wall Street Journal*, April 14, 2017.

2. Bruce Schneier, *Data and Goliath: The Hidden Battles to Collect Your Data and Control Your World* (New York: W.W. Norton and Company, 2015), p. 17.

3. Casey Johnston, "How Chromecast Will Talk to Smartphones Without Wi-Fi or Bluetooth," *Ars Technica*, June 26, 2014, https://arstechnica.com/gadgets/2014/06/chromecast-will-talk-to-smartphones-using-ultrasonic-tones, accessed February 25, 2016.

4. Dan Goodin, "Beware of Ads That Use Inaudible Sound to Link Your Phone, TV, Tablet, and PC," *Ars Technica*, November 13, 2015, https://arstechnica.com/tech-policy/2015/11/beware-of-ads-that-use-inaudible-sound-to-link-your-phone-tv-tablet-and-pc, accessed February 25, 2106.

5. Center for Democracy and Technology, "Comments on Cross-Device Tracking to the FTC," October 16, 2015, https://cdt.org/insight/comments-on-cross-device-tracking-to-the-ftc/, accessed February 25, 2016.

6. Tarun Wadhwa, "Eye-Tracking Technologies Are About to Make Advertising Even More Invasive," *Forbes*, May 8, 2013, https://

213

www.forbes.com/sites/tarunwadhwa/2013/05/08/with-recent -advances-in-eye-tracking-advertising-set-to-become-even-more -invasive/#48256eb92a0c, accessed February 25, 2016.

7. Jayne O'Donnell, "Chronic Sleep Deprivation" *USA Today*, June 1, 2017; interview with Aetna CEO Mark Bertolini, Aetna News, April 5, 2016.

8. Cale Guthrie Weissman, "Cameras at the Water Cooler: Inside the Company That's Always Watching Employees," *Fast Company*, May 25, 2016, https://www.fastcompany.com/3060204/inside-the-company -thats-always-watching-you; Taylor Harris, "Wisconsin Company Offers Employees Microchip Implants," Reuters, July 25, 2017.

9. Bruce Schneier, "Using Law Against Technology," *Schneier on Security*, December 23, 2015, https://www.schneier.com/blog/ archives/2015/12/using_law_again.html (arguing that the current rapid pace of technological change and the complexity of new technologies make it difficult for law to adapt).

Chapter One: What Is the Internet and How Did It Change Data?

1. "History of the AT&T Network," AT&T, http://www.corp.att .com/history/nethistory, accessed February 11, 2016.

2. "Brief History of the Internet Society," Internet Society, https:// www.internetsociety.org/internet/history-internet/brief-history -internet, accessed February 25, 2016.

3. "The OSI Model's Seven Layers Defined and Functions Explained," Microsoft, last reviewed May 13, 2014, https://support.microsoft.com/ en-us/kb/103884.

4. "Requirements for Internet Hosts—Communication Layers," Internet Engineering Task Force, Request for Comments: 1122, October 1989, https://tools.ietf.org/html/rfc1122.

5. "'Cyberscammer' Sentenced to 30 Months for Using Deceptive Internet Names to Mislead Minors to X-Rated Sites," U.S. Department of Justice, February 26, 2004, https://www.justice.gov/archive/ criminal/cybercrime/press-releases/2004/zuccariniSent.htm, accessed February 12, 2016.

6. George Orwell, *1984* (Houghton Mifflin Harcourt, October 1983), pg 2. "The telescreen received and transmitted simultaneously. Any sound that Winston made, above the level of a very low whisper, would be picked up by it, moreover, so long as he remained within the field of vision which the metal plaque commanded, he could be seen as well as heard. There was of course no way of knowing whether you were being watched at any given moment. How often, or on what system, the Thought Police plugged in on any individual wire was guesswork. It was even conceivable that they watched everybody all the time. But at any rate they could plug in your wire whenever they wanted to. *You had to live—did live, from habit that became instinct—in the assumption that every sound you made was overheard, and, except in darkness, every movement scrutinized*" [italics added].

7. "Mobile Data Traffic Surpasses Voice," Ericsson press release, March 23, 2010, http://www.ericsson.com/news/1396928, accessed February 25, 2016.

8. "Visual Networking Index: Global Mobile Data Traffic Forecast Update, 2015–2020," White Paper, Cisco, http://www.cisco.com/c/en/us/solutions/collateral/service-provider/visual-networking-index-vni/mobile-white-paper-c11-520862.html, accessed February 13, 2016.

9. Barry Whyte (orbist), "A Brief History of Areal Density," IBM, September 18, 2009, https://www.ibm.com/developerworks/community/blogs/storagevirtualization/entry/a_brief_history_of_access_density1?lang=en, accessed February 29, 2016.

10. Matt Komorowski, "A History of Storage Cost," September 8, 2009, http://www.mkomo.com/cost-per-gigabyte, accessed February 29, 2016.

11. Rex Farrance, "Timeline: 50 Years of Hard Drives," *PCWorld*, https://www.pcworld.com/article/127105/article.html, accessed February 29, 2016.

12. "Quarterly Retail E-Commerce Sales XX 1st Q. 2017," census.gov.

13. Susannah Fox, "51% of U.S. Adults Bank Online," Pew Research Center, August 7, 2013, www.pewinternet.org/2013/08//07/51-of-u-s-adults-bank-online/.

14. Board of Governors of the Federal Reserve System, *Consumers and Mobile Financial Services 2015*, www.federalreserve.gov/econresdata/consumers-and-mobile-financial-services-report-201503.pdf.

15. Fox, "51% of U.S. Adults Bank Online."

16. Federal Reserve System, "The 2013 Federal Reserve Payments Study," https://www.frbservices.org/assets/news/research/2013-fed-res-paymt-study-summary-rpt.pdf.

17. See Jonathan D. Levin, "The Economics of Internet Markets," National Bureau of Economic Research, January 15, 2012, web.stanford.edu/~jdlevin/Papers/InternetMarkets.pdf.

18. "The Rise of the Sharing Economy," *Economist*, March 9, 2013, https://www.economist.com/news/leaders/21573104-internet-everything-hire-rise-sharing-economy.

19. PricewaterhouseCoopers, *The Sharing Economy* 14 (2015), https://www.pwc.com/us/en/technology/publications/assets/pwc-consumer-intelligence-series-the-sharing-economy.pdf.

20. Elaine Glusac, "As Airbnb Grows, So Do Claims of Discrimination," *New York Times*, June 21 2016; Vauhini Vara, "How Airbnb Makes It Hard to Sue for Discrimination," *New Yorker*, November 3, 2016.

21. Kickstarter, "About Us," https://www.kickstarter.com/about?ref=nav, last visited March 24, 2016.

22. Tax Design Challenge, Challenge.gov, https://www.challenge.gov/challenge/tax-design-challenge, last visited March 24, 2016.

23. "Data, Data Everywhere," *Economist*, February 25, 2010, www.economist.com/node/15557443.

24. *Id.*

25. Desire Athow, "The Data Capacity Gap: Why the World Is Running Out of Data Storage," *Techradar*, February 10, 2015, http://www.techradar.com/news/computing-components/storage/the-data-capacity-gap-why-the-world-is-running-out-of-data-storage-1284024, accessed March 24, 2016.

26. Renee Caruthers, "German Startup Applies Big Data Analytics to Debt Collection," FierceFinanceIT, March 24, 2016, http://www.fiercefinanceit.com/story/german-startup-applies-big-data-analytics-debt-collection/2016-03-24, accessed March 24, 2016.

27. Lindsey Anderson and Irving Wladawsky-Berger, "The 4 Things It Takes to Succeed in the Digital Economy," *Harvard Business Review*,

March 24, 2016, https://hbr.org/2016/03/the-4-things-it-takes-to-succeed-in-the-digital-economy, accessed March 24, 2016.

28. Martin Wilcox, "The Real Reason Why Google Flu Trends Got Big Data Analytics So Wrong," *Forbes*, March 4, 2016, https://www.forbes.com/sites/teradata/2016/03/04/the-real-reason-why-google-flu-trends-got-big-data-analytics-so-wrong/#4ae9287837c0, accessed March 24, 2016.

29. Marc Goodman, *Future Crimes: Everything Is Connected, Everyone Is Vulnerable and What We Can Do About It* (New York: Doubleday, 2015), p. 22.

30. http://www.npr.org/sections/alltechconsidered/2014/05/25/315821415/going-dark-the-internet-behind-the-internet.

31. http://library.cqpress.com/cqresearcher/document.php?id=cqresrre2016011500.

32. https://www.wired.com/2014/11/hacker-lexicon-whats-dark-web.

33. https://www.fas.org/sgp/crs/misc/R44101.pdf.

34. http://library.cqpress.com/cqresearcher/document.php?id=cqresrre2016011500.

35. https://www.wilsoncenter.org/publication/the-deep-web-and-the-darknet.

36. https://darkwebnews.com/darknet-markets/darknet-not-beyond-law.

37. https://www.fas.org/sgp/crs/misc/R44101.pdf.

38. Joshuah Bearman and Tomer Hanuka, "The Rise and Fall of Silk Road, Part I," *Wired*, May 2015, https://www.wired.com/2015/04/silk-road-1.

39. Jamie Bartlett, *The Dark Net* (New York: Melville House, 2015), p. 138.

40. *Id.*, p. 141.

41. https://finance.yahoo.com/news/death-silk-road-darknet-markets-142500702.html.

42. *Id.*

43. *Id.*

44. https://darkwebnews.com/darknet-markets/darknet-not-beyond-law.

45. Izabella Kaminska, "Dark Web Master Thwarted by Love of Old-Fashioned Cash," *Financial Times Weekend*, July 22–23, 2017, https://www.ft.com/content/982a45b0-6e09-11e7-bfeb-33fe0c5b7eaa.

46. http://www.nytimes.com/2013/05/10/nyregion/eight-charged-in-45-million-global-cyber-bank-thefts.html.

47. Francesco Canepa, "SWIFT Network Wasn't Hacked in $81 Million Heist: CEO," Reuters, May 12, 2016, http://www.reuters.com/article/us-bangladesh-heist-swift/swift-network-wasnt-hacked-in-81-million-bangladesh-heist-ceo-idUSKCN0Y320K, accessed May 16, 2016.

48. Rick Gladstone, "Bangladesh Bank Chief Resigns After Cyber Theft of $81 Million," *New York Times*, March 15, 2016, https://www.nytimes.com/2016/03/16/world/asia/bangladesh-bank-chief-resigns-after-cyber-theft-of-81-million.html, accessed May 16, 2016.

49. Michael Corkery, "Hackers' $81 Million Sneak Attack on World Banking," *New York Times*, https://www.nytimes.com/2016/05/01/business/dealbook/hackers-81-million-sneak-attack-on-world-banking.html, accessed May 15, 2016.

50. Jim Finkle, "Bangladesh Bank Hackers Compromised SWIFT Software, Warning Issued," Reuters, April 25, 2016, https://www.reuters.com/article/us-usa-nyfed-bangladesh-malware-exclusiv/bangladesh-bank-hackers-compromised-swift-software-warning-issued-idUSKCN0XM0DR, accessed May 16, 2016.

51. Corkery, "Hackers' $81 Million Sneak Attack."

52. Gladstone, "Bangladesh Bank Chief Resigns."

53. See Nicole Perlroth and Michael Corkery, "North Korea Linked to Digital Attacks on Global Banks," *New York Times*, May 26, 2016, https://www.nytimes.com/2016/05/27/business/dealbook/north-korea-linked-to-digital-thefts-from-global-banks.html.

54. Alex Dobuzinskis and Jim Finkle, "California Hospital Makes Rare Admission of Hack, Ransom Payment," Reuters, February 19, 2016, https://www.reuters.com/article/us-california-hospital-cyberattack/california-hospital-makes-rare-admission-of-hack-ransom-payment-idUSKCN0VS05M, accessed May 17, 2016.

55. Jose Pagliery, "U.S. Hospitals Are Getting Hit by Hackers," CNN, March 28, 2016, http://money.cnn.com/2016/03/23/technology/hospital-ransomware/index.html, accessed May 17, 2016.

56. Selena Larson, "Massive Cyberattack Targeting 99 Countries Causes Sweeping Havoc," CNN Tech, May 13, 2017, http://money.cnn.com/2017/05/12/technology/ransomware-attack-nsa-microsoft/index.html.

57. Craig Timber, "Net of Insecurity: Hacks in the Highway," *Washington Post*, July 22, 2015, http://www.washingtonpost.com/sf/business/2015/07/22/hacks-on-the-highway/?utm_term=.ae5da18806bb, accessed February 5, 2016.

58. Ido Kilovaty, "Want to Keep Hackers Out of Gadgets? Try International Law," *Wired*, February 7, 2017.

59. Kim Zetter, "Xfinity's Security System Flaws Open Homes to Theieves," *Wired*, January 5, 2016,

60. Lily Hay Newman, "Yes, Even Internet-Connected Dishwashers Can Get Hacked," *Wired*, April 1, 2017.

61. Danny Yadron, "Iranian Hackers Infiltrated New York Dam in 2013," *Wall Street Journal*, December 20, 2015, https://www.wsj.com/articles/iranian-hackers-infiltrated-new-york-dam-in-2013-1450662559, accessed May 17, 2016.

62. Shimon Prokupecz and Tal Kopan, "Former Official: Iranians Hacked into New York Dam," CNN, December 22, 2015, http://www.cnn.com/2015/12/21/politics/iranian-hackers-new-york-dam/index.html, accessed May 17, 2016.

63. Joseph Berger, "A Dam, Small and Unsung; Is Caught Up in an Iranian Hacking Case," *New York Times*, March 25, 2016, https://www.nytimes.com/2016/03/26/nyregion/rye-brook-dam-caught-in-computer-hacking-case.html, accessed May 16, 2016.

64. *Id.*

65. Electricity Information Sharing and Analysis Center (E-ISAC), "Analysis of the Cyber Attack on the Ukrainian Power Grid," March 18, 2016, http://www.nerc.com/pa/CI/ESISAC/Documents/E-ISAC_SANS_Ukraine_DUC_18Mar2016.pdf.

66. Kim Zetter, "Inside the Cunning Unprecedented Hack of Ukraine's

Power Grid," *Wired*, March 3, 2016, https://www.wired.com/2016/03/inside-cunning-unprecedented-hack-ukraines-power-grid, accessed May 17, 2016.

67. *Id.*

68. E-ISAC, "Analysis of the Cyber Attack on the Ukrainian Power Grid."

69. Kim Zetter, "Everything We Know About Ukraine's Power Plant Hack," *Wired*, January 20, 2016, https://www.wired.com/2016/01/everything-we-know-about-ukraines-power-plant-hack, accessed May 17, 2016.

70. Jordan Robertson and Michael Riley, "How Hackers Took Down a Power Grid," *Bloomberg*, January 14, 2016, http://www.bloomberg.com/news/articles/2016-01-14/how-hackers-took-down-a-power-grid, accessed May 17, 2016.

71. Industrial Control Systems Cyber Emergency Response Team (ICS-CERT), "Cyber-Attack Against Ukrainian Critical Infrastructure," Alert (IR0-ALERT-H-16-056-021), U. S. Department of Homeland Security, February 25, 2016, https://ics-cert.us-cert.gov/alerts/IR-ALERT-H-16-056-01.

72. FireEye, "Cyber Attacks on the Ukrainian Grid: What You Should Know," https://www.fireeye.com/content/dam/fireeye-www/global/en/solutions/pdfs/fe-cyber-attacks-ukrainian-grid.pdf, accessed May 17, 2016.

73. Zetter, "Everything We Know."

74. Jim Finkle, "US Warns Businesses of Hacking Campaign," Reuters, June 30, 2017, https://www.reuters.com/article/us-usa-cyber-energy/u-s-warns-businesses-of-hacking-campaign-against-nuclear-energy-firms-idUSKBN19L2Z9.

Chapter Two: How Did Law and Policy Evolve to Address Data 1.0 and 2.0?

1. See *Entick v. Carrington*, 19 How. St. Tr. 1029, 95 Eng. Rep. 807 (K.B. 1765).

2. Boyd v. United States, 116 U.S. 616, 625 (1886).

3. *Id.* at 626–27.

4. See generally, Akhil Reed Amar, "The Fourth Amendment, Boston, and the Writs of Assistance," *Suffolk University Law Review* 30 (1996): 53.

5. *Id.* at 76.

6. U.S. Const. amend. IV.

7. Frederick S. Lane, *American Privacy: The 400-Year History of Our Most Contested Right* (Boston: Beacon Press, 2009), p. 65.

8. Roberson v. Rochester Folding Box Co., 64 N.E. 442, 442 (N.Y. 1902).

9. *Id.*

10. *Id.* at 443.

11. *Id.* at 447–48.

12. William L. Prosser, "Privacy," *California Law Review* 48 (1960): 383, 385.

13. Genelle Belmas and Wayne Overbeck, *Major Principles of Media Law* (Wadsworth, 2012), p. 182.

14. Pavesich v. New England Life Insurance Co., 50 S.E. 68, 80 (Ga. 1905).

15. Samuel D. Warren and Louis D. Brandeis, "The Right to Privacy," *Harvard Law Review* 4 (1890): 193.

16. *Id.*

17. Richard F. Hamm, "*Olmstead v. United States:* The Constitutional Challenges of Prohibition Enforcement 1," Federal Judicial Center, 2010, https://www.fjc.gov/sites/default/files/trials/sfj-olmstead_0.pdf.

18. *Id.* at 3.

19. *Id.* at 4.

20. *Id.* at 1–11.

21. Olmstead v. United States, 277 U.S. 438, 463 (1928).

22. *Id.* at 474 (1928) (Brandeis, J., dissenting).

23. Gina Stevens and Charles Doyle, *Privacy: An Overview of Federal Statutes Governing Wiretapping and Electronic Eavesdropping*, Congressional Research Service Report 98-326 (2012), p. 2.

24. Harvey A. Schneider, "*Katz v. United States*: The Untold Story," *McGeorge Law Review* 40 (2009): 13, http://www.mcgeorge.edu/Documents/Publications/06_Schneider_Master1MLR40.pdf. (Schneider was Katz's attorney.)

25. *Id.* at 13–14.

26. *Id.* at 13–23.

27. Katz v. United States, 389 U.S. 347, 351 (1967).

28. David Price, "A Social History of Wiretaps," *CounterPunch*, August 9, 2013, https://www.counterpunch.org/2013/08/09/a-social-history-of-wiretaps-2.

29. "*Olmstead v. United States*: The Constitutional Challenges of Prohibition Enforcement. Minority Opinion on the Appeal of the Olmstead Defendants, U.S. Circuit Court of Appeals for the Ninth Circuit," Federal Judicial Center, http://www.fjc.gov/history/home.nsf/page/tu_olmstead_doc_8.html, accessed May 21, 2016.

30. Neal K. Katyal and Richard Caplan, "The Surprisingly Stronger Case for the Legality of the NSA Surveillance Program: The FDR Precedent," Georgetown University Law Center, March 2008, http://scholarship.law.georgetown.edu/cgi/viewcontent.cgi?article=1058&context=fwps_papers.

31. Sam Roberts, "Judith Coplon, Haunted by Espionage Case, Dies at 89," *New York Times*, March 1, 2011, http://www.nytimes.com/2011/03/02/us/02coplon.html?_r=0.

32. Omnibus Crime Control and Safe Streets Act of 1968, June 19, 1968, Public Law 90-351; 82 Stat. 1978, https://transition.fcc.gov/Bureaus/OSEC/library/legislative_histories/1615.pdf.

33. "Timeline of the C.I.A.'s 'Family Jewels,'" *New York Times*, June 26, 2007, http://www.nytimes.com/2007/06/26/washington/26cia-timeline.html.

34. Seymour M. Hersh, "Huge C.I.A. Operation Reported in U.S. Against Antiwar Forces, Other Dissidents in Nixon Years," *New York Times*, December 22, 1974, http://www.nytimes.com/1974/12/22/archives/huge-cia-operation-reported-in-u-s-against-antiwar-forces-other.html.

35. "The Foreign Intelligence Surveillance Act of 1978," Justice

Information Sharing, https://it.ojp.gov/ PrivacyLiberty/authorities/ statutes/1286, accessed May 20, 2016.

36. "Testimony by Mr. Leahy (for himself and Mr. Mathias)," *Congressional Record—Senate*, September 19, 1985, p. 24365, https://www.justice .gov/sites/default/files/jmd/legacy/2014/07/11/cr-24365-71-1985.pdf.

37. Electronic Communications Privacy Act of 1986, Public Law 99-508; 99th Congress, https://www.gpo.gov/fdsys/pkg/STATUTE -100/pdf/STATUTE-100-Pg1848.pdf.

38. J. K. Peterson, *Handbook of Surveillance Technologies* (New York: CRC Press, 2012), p. 15.

39. *Smith v. Maryland*.

Chapter Three: Data 3.0 and the Challenges of Privacy and Security

1. Rovio Entertainment Ltd. Privacy Policy, Rovio.com.

2. Steve Kroft, "The Data Brokers: Selling Your Personal Information," CBS News, March 9, 2014, http://www.cbsnews.com/news/the-data -brokers-selling-your-personal-information/.

3. Martha T. Moore, "Pa. School District's Web Surveillance Focus of Suit," *USA Today*, March 3, 2010, http://usatoday30.usatoday.com/ tech/news/surveillance/2010-05-02-school-spy_N.htm.

4. "Lower Merion School District Settles Webcam Lawsuits for $610,000," *Huffington Post*, December 11, 2010, http://www.huffingtonpost .com/2010/10/11/lower-merion-school-distr_n_758882.html.

5. Chloe Albanesius, "Pa. School Sued (Again) over Webcam Spying," *PC Magazine*, June 8, 2011, http://www.pcmag.com/article2 /0,2817,2386599,00.asp.

6. Nate Anderson, "School Laptop Spy Case Prompts Wiretap Act Rethink," *Ars Technica*, March 29, 2010, https://arstechnica.com/tech -policy/2010/03/school-laptop-spy-case-prompts-wiretap-act-rethink.

7. ACLU, "Simon Glik Broke No Law When He Used His Cell Phone to Record Police Officers' Use of Force Against Another Man on Boston Common," August 29, 2011, https://www.aclu.org/news/appeals -court-unanimously-affirms-right-videotape-police.

8. Fern Shen, "City to Pay $250,000 to Man Who Says Police Deleted Cellphone Video," *Baltimore Brew*, March 12, 2014, https://www.baltimorebrew.com/2014/03/12/city-to-pay-250000-to-man-who-says-police-deleted-cellphone-video/.

9. "Statement of Interest of the United States," United States District Court for the District of Maryland, January 10, 2012, https://www.rcfp.org/sites/default/files/docs/20120112_173432_federal_filing_on_recording_police.pdf.

10. "Exhibit A. Policy," available at http://www.aclu-md.org/uploaded_files/0000/0487/bpd_policy.pdf, May 25, 2016.

11. Kevin Rector, "Baltimore Police Officers Begin Wearing Body Cameras," *Baltimore Sun*, October 26, 2015, http://www.baltimoresun.com/news/maryland/baltimore-city/bs-md-ci-police-body-worn-cameras-20151026-story.html.

12. Ian Evans, "Report: London No Safer for All Its CCTV Cameras," *Christian Science Monitor*, February 2, 2012, https://www.csmonitor.com/World/Europe/2012/0222/Report-London-no-safer-for-all-its-CCTV-cameras.

13. Olivia J Greer, "No Cause of Action: Video Surveillance in New York City," *Michigan Telecommunications and Technology Law Review* 18, no. 2 (2012): 594, http://repository.law.umich.edu/cgi/viewcontent.cgi?article=1021&context=mttlr.

14. Jeffrey Friedl, "Jeffrey's Exif Viewer," http://exif.regex.info/exif.cgi, accessed March 2, 2016.

15. An example image, which includes GPS metadata, can be found at http://static.panoramio.com/photos/ original/18517440.jpg (image credit: Fred Zahradnik, http://www.panoramio.com/user/2535563, accessed March 2, 2016).

16. Kate Murphy, "Web Photos That Reveal Secrets, Like Where You Live," *New York Times*, August 11, 2010, http://www.nytimes.com/2010/08/12/technology/personaltech/12basics.html, March 2, 2016.

17. Amber Jamieson, "How Social Media Has Created a New Breed of Paparazzi," *New York Post*, November 8, 2015, http://nypost.com/2015/11/08/paparazzi-reveal-secrets-of-tracking-stars-on-social-media.

18. Kashmir Hill, "Celebrity-Stalking Site JustSpotted Just Got Spurned by Twitter," *Forbes*, October 15, 2010, https://www.forbes.com/sites/kashmirhill/2010/10/15/celebrity-stalking-site-justspotted-just-got-spurned-by-twitter/#662aae91670d, accessed March 2, 2016.

19. Greg Sandoval, "Twitter Lowers Boom on New Celeb-Tracking Site," CNET, October 14, 2010, https://www.cnet.com/news/twitter-lowers-boom-on-new-celeb-tracking-site, accessed March 2, 2016.

20. M. G. Siegler, "Google Hires JustSpotted/Scoopler Team to Work on Google+," *TechCrunch*, July 20, 2011, https://techcrunch.com/2011/07/20/google-justspotted/, accessed March 2, 2016.

21. Aaron Taube, "Google Will Now Track Your In-Store Purchases to Figure Out Whether Its Ads Are Effective," *Business Insider*, April 14, 2014, http://www.businessinsider.com/google-tracking-in-store-purchases-2014-4, accessed March 2, 2016.

22. See Sasha Issenberg, "How Obama's Team Used Big Data to Rally Voters," *MIT Technology Review*, December 19, 2012, https://www.technologyreview.com/s/509026/how-obamas-team-used-big-data-to-rally-voters/.

23. Kai Ryssdal, "The New Frontier of Voter Tracking," *Marketplace*, February 10, 2016, https://www.marketplace.org/2016/02/10/business/new-frontier-voter-tracking mc_cid=db1e887d36&mc_eid=88a9f9918f.

24. Evan Selinger, "Opinion: Presidential Campaigns' Thirst for Big Data Threatens Voter Privacy," *Christian Science Monitor*, October 14, 2015, https://www.csmonitor.com/World/Passcode/Passcode-Voices/2015/1014/Opinion-Presidential-campaigns-thirst-for-big-data-threatens-voter-privacy.

25. Federal Trade Commission, "Consumer Generated and Controlled Health Data," May 7, 2014, https://www.ftc.gov/system/files/documents/public_events/195411/consumer-health-data-webcast-slides.pdf, accessed February 26, 2016.

26. Center for Democracy and Technology, "Comments for November 2015 Workshop on Cross-Device Tracking," October 16, 2015, https://cdt.org/files/2015/10/10.16.15-CDT-Cross-Device-Comments.pdf, accessed February 25, 2016.

27. Federal Trade Commission, *Cross Device Tracking: An FTC Staff Report*, January 2017.

28. Jeevan Vasagar, "Kreditech: A Credit Check by Social Media," *Financial Times*, January 19, 2016, http://www.ft.com/intl/cms/s/0/12dc4cda-ae59-11e5-b955-1a1d298b6250.html#axzz41HzZLTby, accessed February 26, 2016.

29. Ellen Rooney Martin, "Driving Exam: How Much Privacy Are Drivers Willing to Give Up for Better Car Insurance Rates?" *ABA Journal*, April 2016, pp. 15–17.

30. See Steve Rosenbush, "The Morning Download: Insurers Say Consumers Resist Tracking Devices in Cars," *Wall Street Journal*, January 11, 2016, http://blogs.wsj.com/cio/2016/01/11/the-morning-download-insurers-say-consumers-resist-tracking-devices-in-cars.

31. Simon Denyer, "China's Big Brother Plan to Rate Its People," *Washington Post*, October 21, 2016.

32. Marc Goodman, *Future Crimes: Everything Is Connected, Everyone Is Vulnerable and What We Can Do About It* (New York: Doubleday, 2015), p. 22.

33. BBC News, "Hackers 'Hit' US Water Treatment Systems," November 21, 2011, http://www.bbc.com/news/technology-15817335, accessed February 26, 2016.

34. Eduard Kovacs, "Hacker Proves Attack on Water Utility in South Houston," November 19, 2011, http://news.softpedia.com/news/Hacker-Proves-Attack-On-Water-Utility-in-South-Houston-235575.shtml, accessed February 26, 2016.

35. Kim Zetter, "A Cyberattack Has Caused Confirmed Physical Damage for the Second Time Ever," *Wired*, January 8, 2015, http://www.wired.com/2015/01/german-steel-mill-hack-destruction/, accessed February 26, 2016.

36. Andy Greenberg, "How an Entire Nation Became Russia's Test Lab for Cyberwar," *Wired*, June 20, 2017.

37. Jose Pagliery, "The Inside Story of the Biggest Hack in History," *CNN Money*, August 5, 2015, http://money.cnn.com/2015/08/05/technology/aramco-hack/index.html.

38. *Id.*

39. Craig Timber, "Net of Insecurity: Hacks in the Highway," *Washington Post*, July 22, 2015, http://www.washingtonpost.com/sf/business/2015/07/22/hacks-on-the-highway, accessed February 5, 2016.

40. Kevin Poulsen, "Hacker Disables More Than 100 Cars Remotely," *Wired*, March 17, 2010, http://www.wired.com/2010/03/hacker-bricks-cars/, accessed February 26, 2016.

41. Andy Greenberg and Kim Zetter, "How the Internet of Things Got Hacked," *Wired*, December 28, 2015, http://www.wired.com/2015/12/2015-the-year-the-internet-of-things-got-hacked, accessed February 26, 2016.

42. Tide Pods and Powder Dash Button, Amazon, http://www.amazon.com/gp/product/B00WJ12MQ8/ ref=as_li_qf_sp_asin_il_tl?ie=UTF8&camp=1789&creative=9325&creativeASIN=B00WJ12MQ8&linkCode=as2&tag=iotlist-20&linkId, accessed March 11, 2016.

43. June Intelligent Oven, June Corporation, https://juneoven.com, accessed March 11, 2016.

44. August Smart Lock, August Corporation, http://august.com/products/august-smart-lock, accessed March 11, 2016.

45. Digital Key, Hilton Honors, http://hhonors3.hilton.com/en/hhonors-mobile-app/digital-key.html, accessed March 11, 2016.

46. Goodman, *Future Crimes*, p. 22.

47. Pierre Thomas and Olivia Katrandjian, "Chinese Hack into US Chamber of Commerce, Authorities Say," ABC News, December 21, 2011, http://abcnews.go.com/International/chinese-hack-us-chamber-commerce-authorities/story?id=15207642, accessed March 7, 2016.

48. Tim Greene, "Chinese Hack on U.S. Chamber Went Undetected for 6 Months" *Network World*, December 21, 2011, http://www.networkworld.com/article/2184263/malware-cybercrime/chinese-hack-on-u-s--chamber-went-undetected-for-6-months, accessed March 7, 2016.

49. Drew Prindle, "Thousands of Belkin WeMo Devices May Be Vulnerable to Hackers: Updated," *Digital Trends*, February 19, 2014, http://www.digitaltrends.com/home/thousands-belkin-wemo-devices-may-vulnerable-hackers.

50. "Home Hacked Home," *Economist*, July 12, 2014, https://www

.economist.com/news/special-report/21606420-perils-connected -devices-home-hacked-home, accessed March 11, 2016.

51. Kim Zetter, "Xfinity's Security System Flaws Open Homes to Thieves," *Wired*, January 5, 2016; Ido Kilovaty, "Want to Keep Hackers Out of Gadgets? Try International Law," *Wired*, February 7, 2017.

52. Samuel Gibbs, "Hackers Can Hijack Wi-Fi Hello Barbie to Spy on Your Children," *Guardian*, November 26, 2015, accessed March 11, 2016.

53. Matt Peckham, "Set Your Printer on Fire? Hackers Can Do What?" *Time*, November 30, 2011, accessed March 11, 2016.

Chapter Four. Reconfiguring Privacy and Security in the Data 3.0 Universe

1. NSA Website Image located at https://nsa.gov1.info/utah-data -center/utah-data-center-entrance.jpg, accessed May 17, 2016.

2. Timothy L. Thomas, *Dragon Bytes: Chinese Information-War Theory and Practice* (Fort Leavenworth, KS: Foreign Military Studies Office, 2004), pp. 44, 45.

3. Joel Brenner, *America the Vulnerable: Inside the New Threat Matrix of Digital Espionage, Crime, and Warfare* (New York: Penguin, 2011), pp. 117, 118.

4. Michele Riley and Jordan Robertson, "Russian Cyber Hacks on US Electoral System Far Wider Than Previously Known," *Bloomberg*, June 20, 2017; Nicole Perlroth, Michael Wines, and Matthew Rosenberg, "Russian Election Hacking Effects, Wider Than Previously Known, Draw Little Scrutiny," *New York Times*, September 1, 2017.

5. Smith v. Maryland, 442 U.S. 735, 737 (1979).

6. *Id.* at 737–39.

7. Justin Jouvenal, "The New Way Police Are Surveilling You: Calculating Your Threat 'Score,'" *Washington Post*, January 10, 2016, https://www.washingtonpost.com/local/public-safety/the-new-way -police-are-surveilling-you-calculating-your-threat-score/2016/01/10/ e42bccac-8e15-11e5-baf4-bdf37355da0c_story.html?utm_ term=.855269fef869, accessed March 11, 2016.

8. Steve Henn, "In More Cities, a Camera on Every Corner, Park and Sidewalk," NPR, June 20, 2013, http://www.npr.org/sections/alltechconsidered/2013/06/20/191603369/The-Business-Of-Surveillance-Cameras, accessed March 22, 2016.

9. "The StingRay's Tale," *Economist*, January 30, 2016, accessed online March 22, 2016, at http://www.economist.com/news/united-states/21689244-courts-take-aim-technology-beloved-countrys-police-forces-secretive.

10. United States v. Jones, 132 S. Ct. 945, 948–49 (2012).

11. *Id.*

12. *Id.* at 945, 957 (Sotomayor, J., concurring).

13. Compare In re Application of the U.S. for Historical Cell Site Data, 724 F.3d 600, 613 (5th Cir. 2013) (finding user had no reasonable expectation of privacy in cell location data) and United States v. Davis, 785 F.3d 498, 518 (same) with In re Application for an Order Directing a Provider of Electronic Communication Service to Disclose Records, 620 F.3d 304, 317 (3d Cir. 2010) (finding third-party doctrine does not apply to cell site location information records and therefore that users have a reasonable expectation of privacy in them).

14. United States v. Graham, No. 12-4659, 2016 WL 3068018 (4th Cir. May 31, 2016).

15. Sascha Meinrath, "Opinion: Court's Location Data Ruling Spells the End of Privacy," *Christian Science Monitor*, June 1, 2016, https://www.csmonitor.com/World/Passcode/Passcode-Voices/2016/0601/Opinion-Court-s-location-data-ruling-spells-the-end-of-privacy.

16. Aaron Smith, *U.S. Smartphone Use in 2015*, Pew Research Center, April 1, 2015, http://www.pewinternet.org/2015/04/01/us-smartphone-use-in-2015/.

17. Timothy Ivory Carpenter v. United States of America, 819 F.3d 880 (3rd Cir. 2016), reh'g en banc denied, cert. granted, __ U.S. __ (June 5, 2017).

18. Riley v. California, 134 S. Ct. 2473 (2014).

19. United States v. Wurie, 728 F.3d 1, 1 (1st Cir. 2013).

20. Riley, 134 S. Ct., at 2480–81.

21. *Id.* at 2494.

22. *Id.* at 2483.

23. *Id.* at 2489.

24. *Id.* ("Because the United States and California agree that these cases involve *searches* incident to arrest, these cases do not implicate the question whether the collection or inspection of aggregated digital information amounts to a search under other circumstances.")

25. Matt Richtel, "Texting and Driving? Watch Out for the Textalyzer," *New York Times*, April 27, 2016, http://mobile.nytimes .com/2016/04/28/science/driving-texting-safety-textalyzer .html?referer=https://www.google.com/.

26. Riley, 134 S. Ct. ("A cell phone search would typically expose to the government far *more* than the most exhaustive search of a house.")

27. *Id.* at 2489–90.

28. *Id.* at 2490–91.

29. Cynthia McFadden, E. D. Cauchi, William M. Arkin, and Kevin Monahan, "American Citizens: U.S. Border Agents Can Search Your Cellphone," NBC News, March 13, 2017, https://www.nbcnews.com/ news/us-news/american-citizens-u-s-border-agents-can-search-your -cellphone-n732746.

30. "CBP Releases Statistics on Electronic Device Searches," United States Customs and Border Protection, April 11, 2017, https://www .cbp.gov/newsroom/national-media-release/cbp-releases-statistics -electronic-device-searches-0.

31. Morgan Chalfant, "Lawmakers Introduce Bill to End Warrantless Phone Searches at Border," *The Hill*, April 4, 2017, http://thehill.com/ policy/cybersecurity/327246-bipartisan-bill-would-end-warrantless -searches-of-digital-devices-at.

32. E. D. Cauchi, "Border Patrol Says It's Barred from Searching Cloud Data on Phones," NBC News, July 12, 2017, https://www.nbcnews.com/ news/us-news/border-patrol-says-it-s-barred-searching-cloud-data -phones-n782416.

33. Compare United States v. Martinez, No. 13CR3560-WQH, 2014 WL 3671271, at *4 (S.D. Cal. July 22, 2014) (holding that a warrantless

search at the border of a cell phone to collect phone numbers and text messages is permissible if supported by reasonable suspicion) with United States v. Kim, No. CR13-0100(ABJ), 2015 WL 2148070, at *22 (D.D.C. May 8, 2015), appeal dismissed (August 14, 2015) (suppressing evidence from warrantless forensic search at the border of a laptop).

34. J. M. Berger, "Tailored Online Interventions: The Islamic State's Recruitment Strategy," *CTC Sentinel* 8, no. 19 (2015): 21–23, https://www.ctc.usma.edu/v2/wp-content/uploads/2015/10/CTCSentinel-Vol8Iss1036.pdf.

35. Rukmini Callimachi, "ISIS and the Lonely Young American," *New York Times*, June 27, 2015, http://www.nytimes.com/2015/06/28/world/americas/isis-online-recruiting-american.html?_r=0.

36. *Id.*

37. Jeff Seldin, "Flow of Foreign Fighters to Iraq, Syria Unrelenting," Voice of America, January 8, 2016, http://www.voanews.com/content/flow-of-foreign-fighters-to-syria-iraq-unrelenting/3135549.html.

38. Berger, "Tailored Online Interventions," 19.

39. Kim Zetter, "Everything We Know About Ukraine's Power Plant Hack," *Wired*, January 20, 2016, http://www.wired.com/2016/01/everything-we-know-about-ukraines-power-plant-hack, accessed March 22, 2016.

40. Jack Cloherty and Pierre Thomas, "'Trojan Horse' Bug Lurking in Vital US Computers Since 2011," ABC News, November 6, 2014, accessed March 22, 2016.

41. See Andi Wilson, Danielle Kehl, and Kevin Bankston, "Doomed to Repeat History? Lessons from the Crypto Wars of the 1990s," Open Technology Institute, June 17, 2015, https://www.newamerica.org/oti/doomed-to-repeat-history-lessons-from-the-crypto-wars-of-the-1990s/.

42. "The Risk of Key Recovery, Key Escrow, and Trusted Third Party Encryption," *Digital Issues* 3 (June 1998), http://www.crypto.com/papers/escrowrisks98.pdf" \h www.crypto.com/papers/escrowrisks98.pdf.

43. Mike McConnell, Michael Chertoff, and William Lynn, "Why the Fear of Ubiquitous Data Encryption Is Overblown," *Washington Post*, July 28, 2015, https://https://www.washingtonpost.com/opinions/

the-need-for-ubiquitous-data-encryption/2015/07/28/3d145952
-324e-11e5-8353-1215475949f4_story.html.

44. Dan Goodin, "Juniper Drops NSA-Developed Code Following New Backdoor Revelations," *Ars Technica*, January 10, 2016, http://arstechnica.com/security/2016/01/juniper-drops-nsa-developed-code-following-new-backdoor-revelations/, accessed March 22, 2016.

45. Joseph Mein, "NSA Says How Often, Not When, It Discloses Flaws," Reuters, November 6, 2015, http://www.reuters.com/article/us-cybersecurity-nsa-flaws-insight-idUSKCN0SV2XQ20151107, accessed March 22, 2016.

46. Gary R Herbert, governor of Utah, "2012 Energy Summit" webpage, http://blog.governor.utah.gov/2012/02/2012-energy-summit/, accessed May 17, 2016.

47. https://nsa.gov1.info/utah-data-center/.

48. See Article L822-2, French Internal Security Code, https://www.legifrance.gouv.fr/affichCodeArticle.do?cidTexte=LEGITEXT0000 25503132&idArticle=LEGIARTI000030935068.

49. See Article L833-6, French Internal Security Code, https://www.legifrance.gouv.fr/affichCode.do?idSectionTA=LEGISCTA0000309 35094&cidTexte=LEGITEXT000025503132&dateTexte=20160324.

50. Joined Cases C293/12, Digital Rights Ireland v. Minister for Communications, Marine and Natural Resources, and C594/12, Landesregierung, Judgment ¶¶ 65–66 (April 8, 2014), ECLI:EU:C:2014:238, http://curia.europa.eu/juris/document/document.jsf?text=&docid=15 0642&pageIndex=0&doclang=EN&mode=req&dir=&occ=first&part =1&cid=738157.

51. United States v. Jones, 132 S. Ct. 945, 961 (2012) (Alito, J., concurring).

52. *Id.* at 956 (Sotomayor, J., concurring).

53. See *id.*

54. Case C362/14, Schrems v. Data Protection Commissioner, Judgment (October 6, 2015), ECLI:EU:C: 2015:650, http://curia.europa .eu/juris/document/document.jsf?text=&docid=169195&pageIndex =0&doclang=en&mode=req&dir=&occ=first&part=1&cid=687686.

55. *Id.* at ¶¶ 94–95.

56. See Fn 41, Ch. 3—supra.

Chapter Five: Data 3.0 and Controls on Private Sector Use of Data

1. Tarasoff v. Regents of the University of California, 17 Cal. 3d 425, 551 P.2d 334 (1976).

2. See Civil Liability of Psychiatrist Arising Out of Patient's Violent Conduct Resulting in Injury to or Death of Patient or Third Party Allegedly Caused in Whole or Part by Mental Disorder, 80 A.L.R. 6th 469 (2012) (cataloging cases).

3. See *Cohen et al. v. Facebook*, Dkt no.s 16-CV-4453, 5158 (NGG) (LB) Memorandum Opinion filed 5/18/17.

4. Michael E. Miller, "Does Facebook Share Responsibility for an American Peace Activist's Brutal Murder in Israel?" *Washington Post*, October 30, 2015, https://www.washingtonpost.com/news/morning -mix/wp/2015/10/30/does-facebook-share-responsibility-for-an -american-peace-activists-brutal-murder-in-israel.

5. See Eugene Volokh, "Lawsuit Tries to Apply Foreign Speech Restrictions in U.S. Court, Hold Facebook Liable for Not Censoring Allegedly Terrorism-Inciting Pages," *Washington Post*, November 12, 2015, https://www.washingtonpost.com/news/volokh-conspiracy/ wp/2015/11/12/lawsuit-tries-to-apply-foreign-speech-restrictions-in -u-s-court-hold-facebook-liable-for-not-censoring-allegedly-terrorism -inciting-pages/?utm_term=.061f2c88547f.

6. See *id.*; 47 U.S.C. § 230(c)

7. 47 U.S.C. § 230(c)(2)(A).

8. April Glaser, "The Internet of Hate," *Slate*, August 30, 2017, https:// slate.com/technology/2017/08/the-alt-right-wants-to-build-its-own -internet.html.

9. Kent Walker, *Working Together to Combat Terrorists Online*, blog .google September 20, 2017.

10. Jen Weedon, William Nuland, and Alex Stamos, *Information Opera- tions and Facebook*, fbnewsroomus.files.wordpress.com.

11. Valery Gerasimov, "The Value of Science Is in the Foresight," reprinted in *Military Review*, January–February 2016, found at usacac .army.mil.

12. Globsec Trends, "Central Europe Under the Fire of Propaganda," September 2016, www.globsec.org; Globsec Policy Institute, Vulnerability Index 2017, www.globsec.org.

13. Elle Hunt, "What Is Fake News," *The Guardian*, December 17, 2016, https://www.theguardian.com/media/2016/dec/18/what-is-fake -news-pizzagate.

14. http://www.dw.com/en/bundestag-passes-law-to-fine-social -media-companies-for-not-deleting-hate-speech/a-39486694.

15. Elena Larina and Vladimir Ovchinskiy, *21st Century Cyberwars: The Russian View* (Bulgaria: Belfort, 2015).

16. Bruce Schneier, *Data and Goliath: The Hidden Battles to Collect your Data and Control Your World* (New York: W.W. Norton and Company, 2015), p. 18.

17. Jonathan Mayer and Patrick Mutchler, "MetaPhone: The Sensitivity of Telephone Metadata," *Web Policy*, March 12, 2014, http:// webpolicy.org/2014/03/12/metaphone-the-sensitivity-of-telephone -metadata/, accessed March 24, 2016.

18. See discussion of *United States v. Jones*, supra, page 111.

19. Thomas Halleck, "How to Turn Off Smartphone Apps That Track You in the Background," *International Business Times*, August 14, 2014, http://www.ibtimes.com/how-turn-smartphone-apps-track-you-back ground-1657868.

20. Gang Wang et al., "Defending Against Sybil Devices in Crowd-sourced Mapping Services," MobiSys 2016, June 25–30, 2016, Singapore, http://www.cs.ucsb.edu/~ravenben/publications/pdf/waze -mobisys16.pdf.

21. "Law Enforcement Wants Police Tracking App Waze Disabled," *US News*, January 26, 2015, available at http://www.usnews.com/ news/articles/2015/01/26/law-enforcement-wants-police-tracking -app-waze-disabled.

22. Google Spain SL; Google Inc. v. Agencia Española de Protección

de Datos; Mario Costeja Gonzalez, Case C-131/12, European Court of Justice Judgment ¶ 14.

23. *Id.* ¶ 15.

24. *Id.* ¶ 16.

25. *Id.* ¶ 17.

26. *Id.* ¶¶ 92–94, 97.

27. "European Privacy Requests for Search Removals," Google (last updated March 24, 2016), https://www.google.com/transparencyreport/removals/europeprivacy/ (last visited March 24, 2016).

28. https://www.cbsnews.com/news/axl-rose-demands-google-take-down-fat-axl-rose-photo/.

29. Tiffany Hsu, "DreamHost Ordered to Release Some Trump Protest Website Data to U.S.," *New York Times*, August 25, 2017.

Chapter Six: Data 3.0 and Sovereignty— A Question of Conflict of Laws

1. Eric Barrett, "Under the Hood: Automated Backups," Facebook, January 14, 2013, https://www.facebook.com/notes/facebook-engineering/under-the-hood-automated-backups/10151239431923920/, accessed February 29, 2016.

2. Comment, "In re Warrant to Search a Certain Email Account Controlled and Maintained by Microsoft Corp.," *Harvard Law Review* 128 (2015): 1019, http://harvardlawreview.org/2015/01/in-re-warrant-to-search-a-certain-email-account-controlled-maintained-by-microsoft-corp/.

3. In re Warrant to Search a Certain E-Mail Account Controlled & Maintained by Microsoft Corp., No. 13- MJ-2814, 2014 WL 4629624, at *1 (S.D.N.Y. August 29, 2014).

4. In re Warrant to Search a Certain E-mail Account, Dkt No. 14-2985 (2d Cir. July 14, 2016).

5. Grant Gross, "Lawmakers Introduce Two Bills to Protect Email Privacy," *ComputerWorld*, February 12, 2015, http://www.computerworld.com/article/2884018/lawmakers-introduce-two-bills-to-protect-email

-privacy.html; S2383 and HR4943 introduced two bills to protect email privacy.

6. Vinod Skreeharsha and Mike Isaac, "Brazil Arrests Facebook Executive in WhatsApp Data Access Case," *New York Times*, March 1, 2016, https://www.nytimes.com/2016/03/02/technology/brazil-arrests -facebook-executive-in-data-access-case.html.

7. See Case C-362/14, Maximillian Schrems v. Data Protection Commissioner, 2015 E.C.R. 650.

8. Joe Miller, "Wikipedia Link Hidden by 'Right to Be Forgotten,'" BBC News, August 4, 2014, http://www.bbc.com/news/technology -28640218.

9. Adi Robertson, "Google Takes Down Links to British Journalism Under 'Right to Be Forgotten' Rule," *Verge*, July 3, 2014, http://www .theverge.com/2014/7/3/5867477/google-takes-down-links-to-british-journalism-under-right-to-be-forgotten.

10. Samuel Gibbs, "Google to Extend 'Right to Be Forgotten' to All Domains Accessed in EU," *Guardian*, February 11, 2016, http://www. theguardian.com/technology/2016/feb/11/google-extend-right-to -be-forgotten-googlecom.

11. Michael Chertoff and Paul Rosenzweig, "A Primer on Globally Harmonizing Internet Jurisdiction and Regulations," CIGI, Chatham House, 2015, https://ourinternet-files.s3.amazonaws.com/ publications/gcig_paper_no10_0.pdf.

Chapter Seven: Cyber Warfare—Deterrence and Response

1. Tom Espiner, "Georgia Accuses Russia of Coordinated Cyberattack," CNET, August 11, 2008, http://www.cnet.com/news/georgia -accuses-russia-of-coordinated-cyberattack/, accessed May 19, 2016.

2. David Hollis, "Cyberwar Case Study: Georgia 2008," smallwars journal.com, available at http://smallwarsjournal.com/blog/journal/ docs-temp/639-hollis.pdf.

3. John Markoff, "Before the Gunfire, Cyberattacks," *New York Times*, August 12, 2008, http://www.nytimes.com/2008/08/13/ technology/13cyber.html?_r=0, accessed May 15, 2016.

4. Hollis, "Cyberwar Case Study."

5. *Id.*

6. *Id.*

7. "Project Grey Goose Phase II Report: The Evolving State of Cyber Warfare" *Greylogic*, March 20, 2009, p. 15, available at http://fserror .com/pdf/GreyGoose2.pdf.

8. Electricity Information Sharing and Analysis Center (E-ISAC), "Analysis of the Cyber Attack on the Ukrainian Power Grid," March 18, 2016, pp. 1–2, http://www.nerc.com/pa/CI/ESISAC/Documents/ E-ISAC_SANS_Ukraine_DUC_18Mar2016.pdf.

9. Andrew Roth, "Ukraine, Russia Face All-Out Trade War as Tensions over Crimea Resurge," *Washington Post*, November 23, 2015, https:// www.washingtonpost.com/world/europe/ukraine-russia-face-all-out -trade-war-as-tensions-over-crimea-resurge/2015/11/23/be728f86 -91ea-11e5-befa-99ceebcbb272_story.html?utm_term=.60bf8b749b10, accessed March 22, 2016.

10. http://docs.house.gov/meetings/HM/HM08/20160225/104505/ HHRG-114-HM08-Wstate-CilluffoF-20160225.pdf.

11. Kim Zetter, "The NSA Acknowledges What We All Fear: Iran Learns from Cyberattacks," *Wired*, February 10, 2016, https://www.wired .com/2015/02/nsa-acknowledges-feared-iran-learns-us-cyberattacks/.

12. David Sanger, *Confront and Conceal: Obama's Secret Wars and Surprising Use of American Power* (New York: Crown Publishers, 2012), p. 188.

13. *Id.*, p. 199.

14. Testimony, House Intelligence Committee, June 21, 2017.

15. Massimo Calabresi, "The Secret History of Election 2016," *Time*, July 31, 2017, pp. 32 39.

16. Compare *Tallinn Manual 1.0* and *Manual 2.0*.

17. U.S. Department of Defense, Office of General Counsel, *Law of War Manual* (2015), p. 994, http://archive.defense.gov/pubs/law-of -war-manual-june-2015.pdf.

18. The U.S. government has taken the position that any illegal use of force can warrant the use of force in self-defense. Under the U.N. Charter, article 2(4) outlaws the "threat or use of force," while article 51 preserves a state's inherent right to self-defense against an "armed

attack." Some international sources interpret these provisions such that the use of force in self-defense is warranted only in response to the gravest illegal uses of force. See *Tallinn Manual on the International Law Applicable to Cyber Warfare* R. 13 cmt. 6 (Michael N. Schmitt, ed., 2013), citing Military and Paramilitary Activities in and Against Nicaragua (Nicar. v. U.S.), Judgment, 1986 I.C.J. Rep. 14, ¶ 191 (June 27). The U.S. government, however, "has taken the position that the inherent right to self-defense potentially applies against *any* illegal use of force. . . . [T]here is no threshold for a use of deadly force to qualify as an 'armed attack' that may warrant a forcible response." U.S. Department of Defense, *Law of War Manual*, p. 1000 n. 31, quoting Harold Hongju Koh, Legal Adviser, U.S. Department of State, International Law in Cyberspace: Remarks as Prepared for Delivery to the USCYBERCOM Inter-Agency Legal Conference (September 18, 2012), reprinted in *Harvard International Law Journal Online* 54, no. 7 (2012).

19. U.S. Department of Defense, *Law of War Manual*, pp. 998–99.

20. *Id.*, p. 997 n. 9.

21. "Advance Policy Questions for the Honorable Ashton Carter: Nominee to Be Secretary of Defense," United States Senate Committee on Armed Services, February 4, 2015, http://www.armed-services.senate.gov/imo/media/doc/Carter_APQs_02-04-15.pdf.

22. Thomas Rid and Ben Buchanan, "Attributing Cyber Attacks," *Journal of Strategic Studies* 38: (2015), pp. 1–2, 4–37.

23. P. W. Singer and Allan Friedman, *Cybersecurity and Cyberwar: What Everyone Needs to Know* (New York: Oxford University Press, 2014), p. 74.

24. William J. Lynn III, "Defending a New Domain," *Foreign Affairs*, September–October 2010, https://www.foreignaffairs.com/articles/united-states/2010-09-01/defending-new-domain.

25. "Defending the Nation from Cyber Attack" speech delivered by U.S. Secretary of Defense Leon E. Panetta to the Business Executives for National Security, New York, October 11, 2012, http://archive.defense.gov/speeches/speech.aspx?speechid=1728.

26. Bob Orr, "Why the US Was Sure North Korea Hacked Sony," CBS News, January 19, 2015, http://www.cbsnews.com/news/why-the-u-s-government-was-sure-north-Korea-hacked-sony/.

27. Singer and Friedman, *Cybersecurity and Cyberwar*, p. 76.

28. Ellen Nakashima, "Following U.S. Indictments, China Shifts Commercial Hacking Away from Military to Civilian Agency," *Washington Post*, November 30, 2015, https://www.washingtonpost.com/world/national-security/following-us-indictments-chinese-military-scaled-back-hacks-on-american-industry/2015/11/30/fcdb097a-9450-11e5-b5e4-279b4501e8a6_story.html?utm_term=.fb9fa76a6f00.

29. Lynn, "Defending a New Domain."

30. Center for Cyber and Homeland Security, *Into the Gray Zone: The Private Sector and Active Defense Against Cyber Threats* (Washington, DC: George Washington University, 2016).

31. Robert M. Lee, "The Sliding Scale of Cybersecurity," SANS Institute, 2015, pp. 9–11, https://www.sans.org/.

32. *Id.* at p. 11.

33. Project Report, "Into the Gray Zone—The Private Sector and Active Defense Against Cyber Threats," October 2016, https://cchs.gwu.edu/sites/cchs.gwu.edu/files/downloads/CCHS-ActiveDefenseReportFINAL.pdf.

34. *See* Thomas Rid, "Cyber War Will Not Take Place," *Journal of Strategic Studies* 35, no. 5 (2011): 14–15.

35. U.S. Const. art. 1, § 8, cl. 11.

36. See Jeremy A. Rabkin and Ariel Rabkin, "To Confront Cyber Threats We Must Rethink the Law of Armed Conflict," *Emerging Threats in National Security Law* 10 (2012), http://media.hoover.org/sites/default/files/documents/EmergingThreats_Rabkin.pdf; see also Paul Rosenzweig, "International Law and Private Actor Active Cyber Defense Measures," *Stanford Journal of International Law* 50, no. 103 (2014): 112.

37. See Curtis A. Bradley and Jack L. Goldsmith, *Foreign Relations Law*, 5th ed. (Wolters Kluwer, 2014), p. 590.

38. See Bas v. Tingy, 4 U.S. (4 Dall.) 37 (1800).

39. See Bradley and Goldsmith, *Foreign Relations Law*, p. 600. Commentators note that modern international law, including the U.N. Charter's restriction on the threat or use of force among nations, has eliminated the traditional function of declaring war and demarcating perfect wars from imperfect wars.

40. Some commentators have encouraged the U.S. government to think creatively on this front. *See* Rabkin and Rabkin, "To Confront Cyber Threats We Must Rethink the Law of Armed Conflict."

41. See Declaration Respecting Maritime Law, April 16, 1856, reprinted in *American Journal of International Law* 1, Supp. 89 (1907), http://www .icrc.org/applic/ihl/ihl.nsf/Article.xsp?action-openDocument& documentId=473FCBOF41DCC63BC12563CD0051492D.

42. Rosenzweig, "International Law and Private Actor Active Cyber Defense Measures."

43. See *id.*, p. 113.

44. Florian Egloff, "Cybersecurity and the Age of Privateering: A Historical Analogy," University of Oxford Cyberstudies Programme Working Paper Series No. 1 (2015), p. 9.

45. See Center for Cyber and Homeland Security, *Into the Gray Zone*, chapter 7, note 30, supra, pp. 28-29.

46. Rosenzweig, "International Law and Private Actor Active Cyber Defense Measures," pp. 103, 112–13.

47. See Michael N. Schmitt et al., *Tallinn Manual 2.0 on the International Law Applicable to Cyber Operations*, Rule 97 (Cambridge: Cambridge University Press, 2017), pp. 428–32.

48. *Id.*, Rule 100, pp. 435–40.

Conclusion. Meeting the Challenge of Data 3.0— Recommendations for Law and Policy

1. "*Olmstead v. United States:* The Constitutional Challenges of Prohibition Enforcement. Dissenting Opinion of Justice Louis D. Brandeis in *Olmstead v. United States*," Federal Judicial Center, http://www.fjc .gov/history/home.nsf/page/tu_olmstead_doc_15.html, accessed May 21, 2016.

2. See, for example, "Who Has Your Back? Protecting Your Data from Government Requests," Electronic Frontier Foundation, https:// www.eff.org/who-has-your-back-government-data-requests-2015, last visited June 6, 2016.

FURTHER READING

Jamie Bartlett
The Dark Net
Melville House 2015

Joel Brenner
*America the Vulnerable: Inside the New Threat Matrix
of Digital Espionage, Crime, and Warfare*
Penguin 2011

Nicholas Burns and Jonathon Price, eds.
Securing Cyberspace
Aspen Institute 2012

Marc Goodman
*Future Crimes: Everything Is Connected,
Everyone Is Vulnerable and What We Can Do About It*
Doubleday 2015

Fred Kaplan
Dark Territory
Simon and Schuster 2016

Alexander Klimburg
The Darkening Web
Penguin 2017

Elena Larina and Vladimir Ovchinsky
21st Century Cyber Wars: The Russian View
Belfort, Bulgaria 2015

Edward Lucas
Cyberphobia
Bloomsbury 2015

David Sanger
Confront and Conceal
Crown 2012

Michael Schmitt
Tallinn Manual 2.0 on the International Law
Approach to Cyber Operations
Cambridge University Press 2017

Bruce Schneier
Data and Goliath
W. W. Norton 2015

Adam Segal
The Hacked World Order
Public Affairs 2016

Andrei Soldatov and Irina Borogan
The Red Web
Public Affairs

Kim Zetter
Countdown to Zero Day
Crown 2014

INDEX